ARABIC PROVERBS

AND

WISE SAYINGS

ARABIC PROVERBS

AND

WISE SAYINGS

Joyce Åkesson

Pallas Athena

Lund

2011

Arabic Proverbs and Wise Sayings

2011 Pallas Athena Distribution, Skarpskyttevägen 10 A, 226 42 Lund, Sweden.

Book design by Joyce Åkesson

ISBN: 978-91-978954-5-3

PRINTED IN THE UNITED STATES OF AMERICA

ALSO BY JOYCE ÅKESSON

Causes and Principles in Arabic, Pallas Athena Distribution, June 2011.

A Study of Arabic Phonology, Pallas Athena Distribution, August 2010.

The Basics & Intricacies of Arabic Morphology, Pallas Athena Distribution, July 2010.

The Phonological Changes due to the Hamza and Weak Consonant in Arabic, Pallas Athena Distribution, April 2010.

A Study of the Assimilation and Substitution in Arabic, Pallas Athena Distribution, March 2010.

The Essentials of the Class of the Strong Verb in Arabic, Pallas Athena Distribution, January 2010

The Complexity of the Irregular Verbal and Nominal Forms & the Phonological Changes in Arabic, Pallas Athena Distribution, April 2009.

Arabic Morphology and Phonology: Based on the Marāḥ al-Arwāḥ by Aḥmad b. ᶜAlī b. Masᶜūd, Studies in Semitic Languages and Linguistics, Brill Academic Publishers, July 2001.

Aḥmad B. ᶜAlī B. Masᶜūd on Arabic Morphology, Marāḥ al-Arwāḥ: Part 1: The Strong Verb, Studia Orientalia Lundensia, Vol. 4, Brill Academic Publishers, October 1990.

POETRY

Majnūn Leyla: Poems about Passion, Pallas Athena Distribution, December 2009.

The Invitation, Pallas Athena Distribution, July 2009.

Love's Thrilling Dimensions, Pallas Athena Distribution, February 2009.

CONTENTS

PREFACE

Proverbs bring color to our speech. A way to understand a foreign culture is to learn its proverbs. This book presents a selection of more than 700 proverbs and wise sayings from the Arabic world. The dialectal forms are changed and presented in Modern Standard Arabic. The Arabic expressions are paralleled with transliterations, translations into English, and often explanations and English equivalents.

The aim of the study is to enlarge the reader's vocabulary in Arabic and to stimulate cross cultural discussions.

Transliteration Pronunciation Guide

Transliteration letter	Arabic letter
ʾalif	ا
bāʾ	ب
tāʾ	ت
ṯāʾ	ث
ǧīm	ج
ḥāʾ	ح
ḫāʾ	خ
dāl	د
ḏāl	ذ
rāʾ	ر
zāl	ز

sīn	س
šīn	ش
ṣād	ص
ḍād	ض
ṭāᵓ	ط
ẓāᵓ	ظ
ᶜayn	ع
ġayn	غ
fāᵓ	ف
qāf	ق
kāf	ك
lām	ل
mīm	م
nūn	ن
hāᵓ	ه
wāw	و
yāᵓ	ي

حرف الألف

The letter "ʾalef"

1

إبن الإبن الحبيب، ابن البنت ابن الغريب

ʾibnu l-ʾibni l-ḥabību, ʾibn l-binti ʾibnu l-ġarībi

The son of the son is the beloved one, the son of the daughter is the stranger's son

2

إبن الحكومة إذا صادقته أكلك واذا عاديته هلكك

ʾibnu l-ḥukūmati ʾiḏā ṣādaqtahu ʾakalaka wa-ʾiḏā ʿādaytahu halakaka

If you befriend a government official he will devour you and if you have any enmity with him he will destroy you

3

إبنك على ما ربيتيه وزوجك على ما عودتيه

ʾibnuki ʿalā mā rabbaytīhi wa-zawǧuki ʿalā mā ʿawwadtīhi

Your son is according to how you have raised him and your husband is according to what you have accustomed him to

Applied to a woman meaning that it is her fault that things are the way they are.

4

إبنك لك بنتك لا

ʾibnuka laka bintuka lā

Your son is yours, your daughter is not

5

إبنه على كتفه ويفتش عليه

ʾibnuhu ʿalā katifihi wa-yufattišu ʿalayhi

His son is on his shoulder and he is looking for him

<u>6</u>

إبنها يبكي وراحت تسكت إبن الجيران

ʾibnuhā yabkī wa-rāḥat tusakkitu bna l-ǧīrāni

Her son is crying and she went to silence the neighbor's son

Applied to someone who sees others' problems and not his or her own.

<u>7</u>

أحد يأخذ الدب إلى كرمته؟

ʾaḥadun yaʾḫuḏu l-dibba ʾilā karmatihi

Is there anyone who takes the bear to his vine?

Applied to someone who shows an opportunist his valuable resources or how he or she makes his or her profit.

<u>8</u>

الأخ جنح

al-ʾaḫu ǧanaḥun

The brother is a wing (i.e. a refuge and assistance)

<u>9</u>

أخذ في وادي جذبات

ʾaḫaḏa fī wādī ǧaḏabāti

He took his way into the valley of Ğezhebāt

Applied to a man who has missed the objet of his aim or pursuit.

10

يأخذ اللين ما يعجز عنه الشديد

yaʾḫuḏu l-laynu mā yaʿǧizu ʿanhu l-šadīdu

Softness wins over what harshness is incapable of winning over

A soft answer turns away wrath

11

يأخذك إلى النهر ويرجعك عطشانا

yaʾḫuḏuka ʾilā l-nahri wa-yuraǧǧiʿuka ʿaṭšānan

He takes you to the river and brings you back thirsty

Said to describe a cunning person who is able to manipulate others.

He can twist you around his little finger

12

خذ وأعط

ḫuḏ wa-ʾaʿṭi

Take and give

Be flexible

13

خذوا أسرارهم من صغارهم

ḫuḏū ʾasrārahum min ṣiġārihim

Take their secrets from their children

14

أداب المرء خير من ذهبه

ʾadābu l-marʾi ḫayrun min ḏahabihi

A person's ethics is better than his gold

15

إذا بليتم فاستتروا

ʾiḏā bulītum fa-statirū

If you get wet, cover yourselves

16

إذا تخاصم اللصان ظهر المسروق

ʾiḏā taḫāṣama l-luṣṣāni ẓahara l-masrūqu

If the two thieves quarreled, the stolen object showed up

17

إذا تم العقل قل الكلام

ʾiḏā tamma l-ʿaqlu qalla l-kalāmu

If the mind were perfect the words would be few

18

إذا أراد ربنا هلاك نملة أنبت لها أجنحة

ʾiḏā ʾarāda rabbunā halāka namlatin ʾanbata lahā ʾaǧniḥatan

If God wanted to kill an aunt he would make wings grow upon her

Said about the destruction of some persons who are incapable of managing their lives when they are elevated to higher positions or better circumstances.

19

إذا أردت السلام فاستعد للحرب

ʾiḏā ʾaradta l-salāma fa-staʿidd li-l-ḥarbi

If you want peace prepare yourself for war

20

إذا تريد أن تحيره خيره

ʾiḏā turīdu ʾan tuḥayyirahu ḫayyirhu

If you wanted to cause confusion in him let him make a choice

21

اذا تريد أن تخرب بلادا إدعي عليها بكثر الرؤساء

ʾiḏā turīdu ʾan tuḫarriba bilādan ʾidʿī ʿalayhā bi-kiṯri l-ruʾasāʾi

If you want to ruin a country, pray that it may have many chiefs

22

إذا راح إلى البحر ينشفه

ʾiḏā rāḥa ʾilā l-baḥri yunaššifuhu

If he goes to the sea, he will cause it to dry

Refers to a person who has bad luck in his undertakings.

23

إذا زل العالم زل بزلته عالما

ʾiḏā zalla l-ʿālimu zalla bi-zillatihi ʿālaman

If the scientist makes a mistake his mistake will have bad effects on a whole world

24

إذا سأل ألحف وإن سئل سوف

ʾiḏā saʾala ʾalḥafa wa-ʾin suʾila sawwafa

When he asks (for something) he insists but when he is asked (for something) he postpones

25

إذا سمعت رجلا يقول فيك من الخير ما ليس فيك
فلا تأمن أن يقول فيك من الشر ما ليس فيك

ʾiḏā samiʿta rağulan yaqūlu fīka mina l-ḫayri mā laysa fīka fa-lā taʾminu ʾan yaqūla fīka mina l-šarri mā laysa fīka

If you hear a person saying good things about you that are not in you, then don't be sure that he would not also say bad things about you that are not in you

26

إذا ضربت فأوجع فإن الملامة واحدة

ʾiḏā ḍarabta fa-ʾawǧiʿ fa-ʾinna l-malāmata wāḥidatun

If you are to hit then cause pain because you'll get the same reproach either way

27

إذا ظلمت من دونك فلا تأمن عقاب من فوقك

ʾiḏā ẓalamta min dūnika fa-lā taʾminu ʿiqāba man fawqika

If you oppress the one who is below you then you will not be safe from the punishment of the one who is above you

28

إذا أعطيت الأعمى عيونك يطمع في حواجبك

ʾiḏā ʾaʿṭayta l-ʾaʿmā ʿuyūnaka yaṭmaʿu fī ḥawāǧibika

If you gave the blind man your eyes he will be greedy to have your eyebrows

Give a clown your finger and he will take your hand

29

إذا تفرقت الغنم قادتها العنز الجرباء

ʾiḏā tafarraqati l-ġanamu qādathā l-ʿinazu l-ğarbāʾu

If the sheep scattered they became led by the scabbed goats

Union is best

30

إذا كثر خناقهم قرب فراقهم

ʾiḏā kaṯura ḫināquhum qaruba firāquhum

If their quarrels increased then their separation is near

31

إذا كثر الطباخون احترقت الطبخة

ʾiḏā kaṯira l-ṭabbāḫūna ḥtaraqati l-ṭabḫatu

If the cooks are many the broth got burnt

Too many cooks spoil the broth

32

إذا كرهك جارك غير باب دارك

ʾiḏā karahaka ǧāruka ġayyir bāba dārika

If your neighbor hates you, change the door of your home

<u>33</u>

إذا أنكسر الجمل حمل حمل الحمار

ʾiḏā nkasara l-ǧamalu ḥammil ḥamla l-ḥimāri

If the camel breaks down, put on a ass-load

Suit your business to your circumstances

<u>34</u>

إذا كان بيتك من زجاج فلا ترمي الناس بالحجارة

ʾiḏā kāna baytuka min zuǧāǧin fa-lā tarmī l-nāsa bi-l-ḥiǧārati

If your own house is made of glass don't throw stones at the people

People who live in glass houses should not throw stones

Don't wash your dirty linen in public

<u>35</u>

إذا كان حبيبك من عسل لا تلحسه كله

ʾiḏā kāna ḥabībuka min ʿasalin lā talḥashu kullahu

If your lover is made of honey do not lick him all up

Moderation is best

36

إذا كان القمر معك لا تبالي بالنجوم

ʾiḏā kāna l-qamaru maʿaka lā tubālī bi-l-nuğūmi

If the moon is with you, do not give importance to the stars

37

اذا كان الكلام من فضة يكون السكوت من ذهب

ʾiḏā kāna l-kalāmu min fiḍḍatin yakūnu l-sukūtu min ḏahabin

If words were of silver then silence is of gold

If speech is silver, silence is golden

38

إذا كان معك نحس لا تسيبه يأتيك أنحس منه

ʾiḍā kāna maʿaka naḥsun lā tuṣībhu yaʾtīka ʾanḥasu minhu

If a worthless fellow (who's like bad luck) is with you, do not let him go or else a worse one will come to you

<u>39</u>

إذا لم يبك الطفل لم ترضعه أمه

ʾiḏā lam yabki l-ṭiflu lam turaḍḍiʿhu ʾummuhu

If the child did not cry his mother would not feed him

<u>40</u>

اذا لم تستح فافعل ما تشاء

ʾiḏā lam tastaḥi fa-fʿal mā tašāʾu

If you have no shame then do whatever you want

Whoever has no regard for others will do as he likes

<u>41</u>

اذا نامت المصيبة فلا تحاول أن توقظها

ʾiḏā nāmati l-muṣībatu fa-lā tuḥāwilu ʾan tūqiẓahā

If the disaster sleeps do not try to awaken it

Do not wake up the sleeping bear

42

إذا هبت رياحك فاغتنمها

ʾiḏā habbat riyāḥuka fa-ġtanimhā

If your wind blows, ride it!

Applies to say that if an opportunity comes your way, take advantage of it.

43

يؤذن في مالطة

yuʾaḏḏinu fī Mālṭat

He calls for prayer in Malta

Applies to someone whose call is fruitless. No one will respond to it.

44

أسد علي وفي الحروب نعامة

ʾasadun ʿalayya wa-fī l-ḥurūbi naʿāmatun

He's a lion against me and an ostrich in wars

Refers to someone who pretends to be brave when there is no danger, but is in reality a coward when there is.

45

الأسد في بلاد الغربة جبان

al-ʾasadu fī bilādi l-ġurbati ğabānun

The lion in a foreign country is a coward

46

الأسد لا يصيد الفئران

al-ʾasadu la yaṣīdu l-fiʾrāna

The lion does not chase mice

47

أصل الشر شرارة

ʾaṣlu l-šarri šarāratun

The origin of evil comes from a little spark

Conflagration stems from a spark

48

أكل البيضة وقشرتها

ʾakala l-bayḍata wa-qišratahā

He ate the egg and its shell

Refers to someone who is too greedy.

49

يأكلون تمري وأرمى بالنوى

ya'kulūna tamrī wa-'urmā bi-l-nawā

They eat my dates and throw the seeds at me

50

أكل عليه الدهر وشرب

'akala ʿalayhi l-dahru wa-šariba

Time has eaten and drank upon him/it

Applies to say that he/it is too old.

51

آكل وشارب ومن الهم هارب

'ākilun wa-šāribun wa-mina l-hammi hāribun

He is eating and drinking and running away from worries

Applied to someone who has what he wants and avoids responsibilities.

52

ألف كلمة جبان ولا كلمة الله يرحمه

ʾalfu kalimati ǧabān wa-lā kalimatu al-lāhu yarḥamuhu

It is better to be called "a coward" a thousand times than to have someone saying: "Rest his soul"

<u>53</u>

أم القاتل تنسي، أم المقتول لا تنسي

ʾummu l-qātili tansī, ʾummu l-maqtūli lā tansī

The mother of the killer forgets, the mother of the killed one does not forget

<u>54</u>

أم الأقوال غلبت أم الأفعال

ʾummu l-ʾaqwāli ġalabat ʾumma l-ʾafʿāli

The mother of words conquered the mother of deeds

Words are mightier than actions

The pen is mightier than the sword

<u>55</u>

آمن من الأرض

ʾāmanu mina l-ʾarḍi

More trustworthy than the earth (in which treasures are securely buried)

56

آمنت يا توما؟

ʾāmanta ya Tūmā?

Do you believe now, O Thomas?

Applied to a person who is slow in accepting obvious truths.

57

الأماني لا تدرك بالتمنيات

al-ʾamānī lā tudraku bi-l-tamannīyāti

Aspirations are not fulfilled by wishes

If wishes were horses, beggars might ride

58

إن دخل الفقر من الباب خرج الحب من الشباك

ʾin daḫala l-fiqru mina l-bābi ḫarağa l-hubbu mina l-šubbāki

If poverty entered from the door, love went out from the window

59

إن تذكر الشيطان يحضر فورا

ʾin taḏkura l-šayṭāna yaḥḍiru fawran

Talk of the Devil, and he is bound to appear

Talk of the wolf and you see his tail

60

إن أردت أن تطا ع فسل ما يستطا ع

ʾin ʾaradta ʾan tuṭāʿa fa-sal mā yustaṭāʿu

If you wish to be obeyed ask for what is possible

If you wish to be obeyed don't ask the impossible

61

إن زاد الشيء عن حده ينقلب لضده

ʾin zāda l-šayʾu ʿan ḥaddihi yanqalibu li-ḍiddihi

If something increases more than it should, it will turn against itself

Moderation is best

<u>62</u>

إن كبر ابنك آخيه

ʾin kabira bnuka ʾāḫīhi

When your son grows up, become a brother to him

The teacher learns also from the students

<u>63</u>

إن كنت تدري فتلك مصيبة وإن كنت لا تدري فالمصيبة أعظم

ʾin kunta tadrī fa-tilka muṣībatun wa-ʾin kunta lā tadrī fa-l-muṣībatu ʾaʿẓamu

If you know then it is a disaster, and if you don't know then the disaster is bigger

<u>64</u>

إن كنت ريحا فقد لاقيت إعصارا

ʾin kunta rīḥan fa-qad laqayta ʾiʿṣāran

If you're a wind then you have met a hurricane (in me)

65

إن كنت كذوبا فكن ذكورا

ʾin kunta kaḏūban fa-kun ḏakūran

If you were a liar then you better have a good memory

No man has a good enough memory to make a successful liar

66

أن تصل متأخرا خير من أن لا تصل أبدا

ʾan tasila muta'aḫḫiran ḫairun min ʾan la tasila abadan

That you arrive late is better than that you do not arrive at all

Better late than never

67

أنا أمير وأنت أمير ومن يسوق الحمير

anā ʾamīrun wa-ʾanta ʾamīrun wa-ma yasūqu l-ḥamīra

If I am a prince and you are a prince, then who is leading the donkeys?

68

أنا الغريق فما خوفي من البلل

ʾanā l-ġarīqu fa-mā ḫawfī mina l-balali

It is I who am drowning so I am not afraid of getting wet

69

أنا نقطة في بحرك

ʾanā nuqṭatun fī baḥrika

I am a drop in your sea

Is said to a person who is very knowledgeable in order to show him or her respect.

70

أنا وأخي على ابن عمي، أنا و ابن عمي على الغريب

ʾanā wa-ʾaḫī ʿalā bni ʿammī, ʾanā wa-bnu ʿammī ʿalā l-ġarībi

Me and my brother against my cousin, Me and my cousin against a stranger

Blood is thicker than water

71

أنا وأنت والزمن طويل

ʾanā wa-nta wa-l-zamanu ṭawīlun

(Here) I am and here you are and life is long

I will get you sooner or later

72

إن أخاك من واساك

ʾinna ʾaẖāka man wāsāka

Your brother is he who consoles you

73

إن البعوضة تدمي مقلة الأسد

ʾinna l-baʿʿūḍata tudmī miqlata l-ʾasadi

A mosquito can make the lion's eye bleed

Little enemies and little wounds must not be despised

74

إن الحديد بالحديد يفلح

ʾinna l-ḥadīda bi-l-ḥadīdi yuflaḥu

Iron with iron is cut

Diamond cuts diamond

Fight fire with fire

75

إن الغريق بكل حبل يعلق

ʾinna l-ġarīqa bi-kulli ḥablin yaᶜliqu

A sinking man will try to catch any rope

A desperate person in a difficult situation will do anything to get out of it.

Any port in a storm

76

إن الغصون إذا قومتها اعتدلت

ʾinna l-ġuṣūna ʾiḏā qawwamtahā ᶜtadalat

Twigs if corrected can be rectified

Knowledge is better acquired at a young age

77

إن اللبيب من الإشارة يفهم

ʾinna l-labība mina l- išārati yafhamu

The wise man understands from a sign

A word to a wise man is enough

78

إنك تضرب في حديد بارد

ʾinnaka taḍribu fī ḥadīdin bāridin

You are striking while the iron is cold

Applied to a person who hopes for a matter of which the attainment is improbable or remote.

You cannot change it

79

إنك لا تجني من الشوك العنب

ʾinnaka lā taǧnī mina l-šawki l-ʿanaba

You don't reap grapes from thistles (cactus)

Said to someone who is waiting for a favor from the wrong person.

80

إنما العبرة بالنهاية

ʾinnamā l-ʿibrata bi-l-nihāyati

Better late than never

81

إياك أن يضرب لسانك عنقك

ʾiyyāka ʾan yaḍriba lisānuka ʿunqaka

Beware that your tongue might cut your neck!

Watch out what you say

حرف الباء

The letter “bāʾ”

82

بفلوسك ومالك تنال الذي في بالك

bi-fulūsika wa-mālika tanālu l-laḏī fī bālika

With your money and riches you get what you have in mind

83

بقدر الرأي تعتبر الرجال وبالآمال ينتظر المال

bi-qadari l-raʾyi tuʿtabaru l-riğālu wa-bi-l-ʾāmāli yuntaẓaru l-mālu

By the strength of their opinion men are judged and by hopes money is awaited

84

بنفسي فخرت لا بجدودي

bi-nafsī faḫartu lā bi-ğudūdī

I take pride in myself and not in my ancestors

85

بااللطف تفتح جميع الأبواب

bi-l-luṭfi tuftaḥu ğamīʿu l-ʾabwābi

With kindness all doors open

86

بوجهين ولسانين

bi-wağhayni wa-lisānayni

He has two faces and two tongues

Applied to a hypocrite.

Two-faced

87

بئس الشعار الحسد

biʾsu l-šiʿāri l-ḥasadu

The worst emotion is envy

88

البخيل هو جامع المال لأحفاده

al-baḫīlu huwa ğāmiʿu l-māli li-ʾaḥfādihi

The stingy person is the one who is saving money to his or her grandchildren

89

بدل الشيشة والدخان استر جسمك يا عريان

badalu l-šīšati wa-l-duḫḫāni stur ǧismaka yā ᶜaryāna

Instead of the shisha and the cigarettes, cover your body, O naked one!

90

بصلة الحبيب عند المحب خروف

baṣlatu l-ḥabībi ᶜinda l-muḥibbi ḫarūfun

The onion offered by the beloved is a roast lamb by the loving one

It is the thought that counts

91

بطيخ يكسر بعضه

baṭṭīḫun yukassiru baᶜḍahu

Let the watermelons break each other!

Said to encourage someone not to interfere in others' conflicts.

Let them stew in their own juice

92

البطن لا تلد عدوا

al-baṭnu lā talidu ᶜaduwwan

The belly does not give birth to an enemy

Applied to strengthen the idea of family. A mother gives birth to a member of the family.

93

البعد جفاء

al-buᶜdu ǧafāʾun

Distance is disaffection

94

البعد يزيد القلب ولوعا

al-buᶜdu yazīdu l-qalba wulūᶜan

Absence makes the heart grow fonder

95

بعد السماء من الأرض

bu^c^du l-samā^ɔ^i mina l-^ɔ^arḍi

As far as the heavens/sky is from the earth

96

بعد الضيق الفرج

ba^c^da l-ḍīqi l-farağu

After hardships comes the release from worries

After a storm comes sunshine

97

بعد ما كانت خادمة صارت في البيت حاكمة

ba^c^da mā kānat ḫādimatan ṣārat fī l-bayti ḥākimatan

After having been a servant, she became a ruler in the house

98

إبعد من الشر وغني له

^ɔ^ib^c^id mina l-šarri wa-ġannī lahu

Stay away from trouble (evil) and sing to it

Applied to say to someone to stay away from evil people and troublesome situations and be happy.

Never trouble trouble till trouble troubles you

99

البعيد عن العين بعيد عن القلب

al-baʿīdu ʿani l-ʿayni baʿīdun ʿani l-qalbi

Out of sight, out of mind

100

بعض العفو ضعف

baʿḍu l-ʿafwi ḍiʿfun

Some forgiveness is weakness

101

أبلط اللص القوم

ʾablaṭa l-liṣṣu l-qawma

The robber left the people upon the surface of the ground and left them with nothing

<u>102</u>

بنت الدار عوراء

bintu l-dāri ᶜawrāʾun

The girl of the house is squint-eyed

Applied to say that the person will not be considered good-looking or clever in his or her own home or country.

A prophet is not without honor save in his own country

<u>103</u>

البنت لأمها والصبي لأبيه

al-bintu li-ʾummihā wa-l-ṣabiyyu li-ʾabīhi

The girl is to her mother and the boy is to his father

<u>104</u>

يبني علاليا وقصورا في الهواء

yabnī ᶜalālayā wa-quṣūran fī l-hawāʾī

He builds high chambers and castles in the air

Building castles in Spain

105

يبني قصرا ويهدم مصر

yabnī qaṣran wa-yuhaddimu Miṣra

He builds a castle and destroys Egypt

Applies to a person who puts his or her own interests before anyone else's.

106

الباب الذي يأتي منه ريح سده واستريح

al-bābu l-laḏī ya'tī minhu rīḥun sidhu wa-starīḥ

The door from which the winds comes from, close it and be tranquil

Meant to say get rid of the source of discomfort and make no more ado about it.

107

البيت الذي ليس فيه أولاد صغار ليس فيه نور

al-baytu l-laḏī laysa fīhi 'awlādun ṣiġārun laysa fīhi nūrun

The house in which there are no small children has no light

108

باءت عرار بكحل

bā'at ʿArāri bi-Kaḥlin

ʿArār became slain for Kaḥl

This proverb stems from the story of two cows, which smote each other with their horns until they both died. The proverb is applied to any two that become equal.

109

بيت المرء قلعته

baytu l-mar'i qalʿatuhu

A man's house is his castle

110

بيض وجهه

bayyaḍa waǧhahu

He whitewashed his face

Applied to someone who does a good deed that brings honor.

111

بيضة اليوم خير من دجاجة الغد

bayḍatu l-yawmi ḫayrun min dağāğati l-ġadi

Today's egg is better that tomorrow's chicken

112

باع كرمه واشترى معصرة

bāᶜa karmahu wa-štarā maᶜṣaratan

He sold his vineyard and bought a squeezer

113

بيت بلا امرأة كأنه مقبرة

baytun bi-lā mraᵓatin kaᵓannahu maqbaratun

A house without a woman is like a graveyard

114

بين أربع حيطان

bayna ᵓarbaᶜa ḥīṭāni

Between four walls

Applies for someone who does not get out much.

115

يتباهوا بحالهم ويحسدوا جارهم

yatabāhū bi-ḥālihim wa-yaḥsidū ǧārahum

They boast of their situation and they envy their neighbor

حرف التاء

The letter "tā'"

116

تاجرنا بالأكفان بطلت الناس تموت

tāğarnā bi-l-ʾakfāni baṭṭalati l-nāsu tamūtu

When we started trading coffins, the people stopped dying

Applied to refer to a person who is unlucky in business.

117

تحت السواهي دواهي

taḥta l-sawāhī dawāhī

Still waters run deep

Said of a person who hides cleverness or passion behind his or her shyness or silence.

118

يترك الحمار ويمسك بالبردعة

yatriku l-ḥimāra wa-yamsiku bi-l-bardaᶜati

He leaves the donkey and holds on to the saddle

Said of people who don’t face their match and pick on someone weaker instead.

119

إترك الشر يتركك

ʾitriki l-šarra yatrikuka

Leave evil and it will leave you

120

تركته على مثل مشفر الأسد

taraktuhu ͨalā miṯli mišfari l-ʾasadi

I left him at the like of the lip of the lion

Applied to say that I left him exposed to destruction.

121

ترك الجواب على الجاهل جواب

tarku l-ǧawābi ͨalā l-ǧāhili ǧawābun

Leaving the answer to the ignorant is an answer

122

التفاحة العفنة تفسد جاراتها

al-tuffāḥatu l-ᶜafnatu tafsudu ǧārātahā

The rotten apple damages its neighbors

<u>123</u>

تيس الجبل ولا فيلسوف المدينة

taysu l-ǧabali wa-lā faylasūfu l-madīnati

Better (to frequent) the goat of the mountain than the philosopher of the town

حرف الثاء

The letter "ṯāʾ"

124

ثلاثة لا يخفى: الحب والحمل والركوب على الجمل

ṯalāṭatun lā yuḫfā: al-ḥubbu wa-l-ḥamalu wa-l-rukūbu ͨalā l-ğamali

Three things cannot be hidden: love, pregnancy and riding a camel

125

ثلاثة لا يعار: البارودة والإمرأة والفرس

ṯalāṯatun lā yuͨāru: al-bārūdatu wa-l-ʾimraʾatu wa-l-farasu

Three things cannot be borrowed: the rifle, the wife and the horse

حرف الجيم

The letter "ǧīm"

126

أجدى من الغيث في أوانه

ʾaǧdā mina l-ġayṯi fī ʾawānihi

More profitable than rain in its season

127

جذها جذ العير الصليانة

ǧaḏḏahā ǧaḏḏa l-ʿayra l-Ṣillayānata

He hastened to it/her as the ass hastens to the plant called al-Sillayānat

128

جرب ولاحظ تكن عارفا

ǧarrib wa-lāḥiẓ takun ʿārifan

Experience and observe and you'll become knowledgeable

129

جرح الكلام أعمق من جرح السيوف

ǧirḥu l-kalāmi ʾaʿmaqu min ǧirḥi l-suyūfi

The wound caused by words is deeper than the wound caused by swords

130

جزاء المعروف سبع كفوف

ǧazāʾu l-maʿrūfi sabʿa kufūfin

The reward of being of assistance is getting seven slaps

Ingratitude is the world's reward

131

الجزاء من جنس العمل

al-ǧazāʾu min ǧinsi l-ʿamali

The reward is of the nature of the work

You reap what you sow

132

جسم بغل وعقل سخل

ǧismu baġlin wa-ʿaqlu saḫlin

The body of a mule and the mind of a little goat

Applied to someone with a big body and the mind of a child.

<u>133</u>

جلبت جلبة ثم أمسكت

ğalabat ğalbatun ṯumma ᵓamsakat

A cloud thundered then refrained from raining

Applied to a coward who threatens and then is silent.

<u>134</u>

جلدة على عظمة

ğildatun ᶜalā ᶜaẓmatin

Skin on a bone

All skin and bone / a bag of bones

<u>135</u>

أجمع من الأرض

ᵓağmaᶜu mina l-ᵓarḍi

More comprehensive than the earth

136

المجتمع السيئ يفسد الأخلاق الحميدة

al-muğtamaᶜu l-sayyiᵓu yafsidu l-ᵓaẖlāqa l-ḥamīdata

A bad society corrupts good manners

137

الجمال جمال النفس

al-ğamālu ğamālu l-nafsi

Beauty is the beauty of the soul

Beauty is skin deep

138

الجمال في عين الناظر

al-ğamālu fī ᶜayni l-nāẓiri

Beauty is in the eye of the beholder

139

الجمال قوة والبسمة سيفها

al-ğamālu quwwatun wa-l-basmatu sayfuhā

Beauty is power and the smile is its sword

140

الجاني لك الخير من يجني عليك الشر

al-ğānī laka l-ḫayri ňman yağnī ᶜalayka l-šarra

The person who brings you good is he who brings upon you evil

Applied as a caution, for the Arabs suspect that a benefactor can have some bad intentions.

141

جوابه تحت باطه

ğawābuhu taḥta bāṭihi

His answer is under his armpit

Said to describe a witty person.

142

الجود بالنفس أقصى غاية الجود

al-ğawdu bi-l-nafsi ᵓaqṣā ġāyati l-gawdi

Giving the soul is the ultimate aim of giving

The best gift comes from the heart.

143

أجود من الجواد المبر

ʾağwadu mina l-ğawādi l-mubirri

More swift than the horse that surpasses others

<u>144</u>

الجار قبل الدار

al-ğāru qabla l-dāri

The neighbor comes before the home

Neighbors are important in Arab countries. This is why in order to be happy, it is important to choose good neighbors.

<u>145</u>

جارك صبحه ومسيه والذي في بالك إخفيه

ğāruka ṣabbiḥhu wa-massīhi wa-l-laḏī fī bālika ʾiḫfīhi

Your neighbor, tell him "good morning" and "good evening", and what you have in mind conceal it (from him)

<u>146</u>

جارك القريب ولا أخوك البعيد

ğāruka l-qarību wa-lā ʾakhūka l-baᶜidu

Better your close neighbor than your distant brother

A good neighbor is a found treasure.

147

جارتك الطيبة كأختك البعيدة

ğāratuka l-ṭayyibatu ka-ʾuḫtika l-baʿidati

Your nice female neighbor is like your sister who is far away

148

جاور السعيد تسعد

ğāwiri l-saʿīda tasʿadu

Be a neighbor with the happy man and you will be happy

Keep good company and you shall be of the number

149

جوع قطك يتصيد فأرك وشبع كلبك يحرسك

ğawwiʿ qiṭṭaka yataṣayyadu faʾraka wa-šabbiʿ kalbaka yaḥrisuka

Let your cat be hungry and it will chase your mouse and let your dog be satiated and it will guard you

150

الجوع كافر

al-ǧūᶜu kāfirun

Hunger is an infidel

The meaning of this proverb is that a hungry man can turn into an infidel.

Hunger pierces stone walls

A hungry man is an angry man

151

جاء الخروف يعلم أباه الرعي

ǧāʾa l-ḫarūfu yuᶜallimu ʾabāhu l-raᶜya

The sheep came to teach his father how to graze

Teach your mother to suck eggs

152

جاءت العزبة تشكي لقيت المتجوزة تبكي

ǧāʾati l-ᶜazbatu taškī laqiyati l-mutazawwiǧata tabkī

The single woman came to complain and she found the married woman crying

Everyone has problems, some are just better at hiding them.

153

جاء يكحلها وعماها

ǧāʾa yukaḥḥiluhā wa-ʿamāhā

He came to apply kohl to the eye and blinded it

Kill them with kindness

حرف الحاء

The letter "ḥāʾ"

154

الحب ستار العيوب

al-ḥubbu sattaru l-ᶜuyūbi

Love conceals the defects

Love is blind

155

الحب أعمى

al-ḥubbu ʾaᶜmā

Love is blind

156

حبيبك من تحبه ولو كان قردا

ḥabībuka man tuḥibbuhu wa-law kāna qirdan

Your beloved is the one you love, even if he was a monkey

Love is blind

157

حبة تثقل الميزان

ḥabbatun tuṯaqqilu l-mīzāna

A grain makes the balance heavier

A little thing can decide the strength when it concerns two parties of equal power.

158

حبر على ورق

ḥibrun ᶜalā waraqin

Ink on paper

Applied to say that an agreement has no value.

159

حبل الكذب قصير

ḥablu l-kiḏbi qaṣīrun

The rope of lies is short

160

حبلة ومرضعة وأمامها أربعة

ḥiblatun wa-muraḍḍiᶜatun wa-ᵓamamahā ᵓarbaᶜatun

She is pregnant and breast-feeding a child and has four children before her

Said about the abundance of riches by someone.

161

حج والناس راجعون

ḥağğa wa-l-nāsu rāği^c^ūna

He went to Hajj while pilgrims were coming back

Refers to someone who is late in doing things.

162

إحذر عدوك مرة واحذر صديقك ألف مرة

^ɔ^iḥḏar ^c^aduwwaka marratan wa-ḥḏar ṣadīqaka ^ɔ^alfa marratin

Beware of your enemy once and beware of your friend thousand times

Applies to warn a person that a friend knows more his or her secrets than an enemy does and can therefore hurt him or her more.

163

أحذر من الغراب

ʾaḥḏaru mina l-ġurābi

More cautious than the raven

164

أحذم من حرباء

ʾaḥḏamu min ḥirbāʾin

More prudent than a chameleon

165

حرسوا القط على اللبن

ḥarrasū l-qiṭṭa ʿalā l-labani

They set the cat to guard the milk

They set the wolf to guard the sheep

166

الحركة بركة

al-ḥarakatu barakatun

Movement is a blessing

Meant to say that taking action is positive.

167

تحسبها حمقاء وهي باخس

taḥsibuhā ḥamqāʾun wa-hiya bāḫisun

You think that she is stupid, but she is wrongful or unjust

Refers to a person who feigns himself or herself to be of weak understanding while he or she is crafty and cunning. The proverb stems from the story of a man of the Banū l-ᶜAmbar of Tamīm who wanted to take over the property of a woman, believing that she was stupid enough to be fooled by him, so he combined his property with hers. After mixing and dividing both properties, the woman was not content with the division until she took back her property. She also complained of him to those in authority, so that he was reproved for cheating a woman. He then replied with these words that became a proverb

168

حاسبني مشمشة كل ساعة تهز فيّ؟

ḥāsibunī m̌ušmušatan kullu sāᶜatin tahizzu fiyya?

Do you think that I am an apricot tree that you shake me every hour?

Applied to a person who is annoyed by someone else's irritating manners and demands.

169

حسدوا الفقيرة على الحصيرة

ḥasadū l-faqīrata ᶜalā l-ḥaṣīrati

They envied the poor woman for her rug

Applied to envious persons.

170

يحسدون الأعمى على كبر عيونه

yaḥsidūna l-ᵓaᶜmā ᶜalā kibri ᶜuyūnihi

They envy the blind man for the big size of his eyes

Applied to envious persons.

171

الحاسد يرى زوال نعمتك نعمة عليه

al-ḥāsidu yarā zawāla niᶜmatika niᶜmatan ᶜalayhi

The envious considers the loss of your blessing as a blessing for himself

172

الحسود لا يسود

al-ḥasūdu lā yasūdu

The envious will not prevail

Envy eats nothing but its own heart

173

الإحسان يبدأ بالأهل

al-ʾiḥsānu yabdaʾu bi-l-ʾahli

Charity begins with one's relatives

Charity begins at home

174

يحصد المرء ما زرع

yaḥṣudu l-marʾu mā zaraʿa

As you sow, so you shall reap

175

حظه من السماء الذي تحبه حماته

ḥaẓẓuhu mina l-samāʾi l-laḏī tuḥibbuhu ḥamātuhu

His luck is from heaven, he who is loved by his mother-in-law

176

إحفظ قرشك الأبيض ليومك الأسود

ʾiḥfaẓ qiršaka l-ʾabyaḍā li-yawmika l-aswadi

Keep your white penny for a black day

Save it for a rainy day

177

حفظ الاموال أهون من حفظ الاسرار

ḥafẓu l-ʾamwāli ʾahwanu min ḥafẓi l-ʾasrāri

It is easier to keep money than to keep secrets

178

تحكي بالشرق، يجاوبك بالغرب

taḥkī bi-l-šarqi, yuğāwibuka bi-l-ġarbi

You speak to him about the East, he replies to you about the West

Said of an unfocused person who doesn't listen to what you're saying.

179

يحل ويربط

yaḥillu wa-yarbiṭu

He unties and he ties

Said about a mighty person who is able to solve others' problems.

He pulls the strings

<u>180</u>

حلم القطط كله فئران

ḥilmu l-qiṭaṭi kulluhu fiʾrānun

The dream of the cats is all about mice

<u>181</u>

حلو اللسان بعيد الإحسان

ḥilū l-lisāni baʿīdu l-ʾiḥsāni

Sweet of tongue but far distant in doing good deeds

Said of a hypocrite.

<u>182</u>

الحمد لله الذي أبدلني الدرهم بدينار

al-ḥamdu li-l-lāhi l-laḏī ʾabdalanī l-dirhama bi-dīnārin

Praise be to God who made me change the dirham into a dīnār

Said of a man who divorced and got another better wife.

183

حمار حملوه كتبا حسب نفسه أنه أصبح يقرأ

ḥimārun ḥammalūhu kutuban ḥasiba nafsahu ʾannahu ʾaṣbaḥa yaqraʾu

They loaded the donkey with books; he thought that he was able to read

184

الحمار القصير كالجحش كل من جاء يركبه

al-ḥimāru l-qaṣīru ka-l-ǧaḥši kullu man ǧāʾā yarkabuhu

The short ass is like a donkey, everyone who comes rides it

Applies to someone who does not have a strong personality.

185

حماري ولا حصان جاري

ḥimārī wa-lā ḥiṣānu ǧāri

Better using my own donkey than my neighbor's horse

186

حمارتك العرجاء ولا تسأل اللئيم

ḥimāratuka l-ᶜarǧāᵓu wa-lā tasᵓalu l-laᵓīma

Rather (be satisfied with) your own limp female donkey than asking (a favor) from a cunning person

187

الحماس بلا معرفة نور بلا ضياء

al-ḥamāsu bi-lā maᶜrifatin nūrun bilā ḍiyāᵓin

Zeal without knowledge is fire without light

188

أحمق من راعي ضأن ثمانين

ᵓaḥmaqu min rāᶜī ḍaᵓnin ṯamānīna

More stupid than a pastor of eighty sheep

This proverb stems from a story about an Arab of the desert who announced to Kisrā an event that rejoiced him, whereupon Kisrā said, "Ask of me whatever you want". So the man asked of him to give him eighty sheep when he had the opportunity to ask for much more.

189

أحمق من صاحب ضأن ثمانين

ʾaḥmaqu min ṣāḥibi ḍaʾnin ṯamānīna

More stupid than an owner of eighty sheep

This is a variant of the proverb above (188).

190

أحمق من طالب ضأن ثمانين

ʾaḥmaqu min ṭālibi ḍaʾnin ṯamānīna

More stupid than a demander of eighty sheep

This is a variant of the proverb above (188).

191

حامل السلم بالعرض

ḥāmilu l-sillami bi-l-ʿarḍi

He is carrying the ladder sideways

Applied to a person who has problems in performing a task or who complicates unnecessarily easy matters.

192

حاميها حراميها

ḥāmīhā ḥarāmīhā

The ones who are protecting her are the ones who are robbing her

Trusting the lamb under the care of the wolf

193

الحاجة أم الاختراع

al-ḥāǧatu ʾummu l-ʾiḫtirāʿi

Necessity is the mother of invention

<u>حرف الخاء</u>

<u>The letter "ḫāʾ"</u>

<u>194</u>

أخبرته بعجري وبجري

ʾaḫbartuhu bi-ʿuğarī wa-buğarī

I told him about my vices, (which I concealed from others, by reason of my confidence in him)

<u>195</u>

الأخبار الحسنة تمشي والأخبار السيئة تجري

al-ʾaḫbāru l-ḥasanatu tamšī wa-l-ʾaḫbāru l-sayyiʾatu tağrī

Good news walk, bad news circulate

Bad news sells better than good news

<u>196</u>

خادم سيدين يكذب على أحدهما

ḫādimu sayyidayni yakḏibu ʿalā ʾaḥadihimā

A servant who has two masters lies to one of them

197

خذه بالموت حتى يرضى بالحمى

ḫuḏhu bi-l-mawti ḥattā yarḍā bi-l-ḥimmā

Treat him by showing him death so that he will be content with fever

Applied to say that if you threaten a person with the worst alternative he or she will accept the bad one.

198

أخرس عاقل خير من جاهل ناطق

ʾaḫrasun ʿāqilun ḫayrun min ǧāhilin nāṭiqin

An intelligent mute is better than an ignorant person who can talk

199

أخطب لبنتك ولا تخطب لابنك

ʾaḫṭib li-bintika wa-lā taḫṭibu li-bnika

Work for the engagement of your daughter, but do not work for the engagement of your son

200

خاطب الناس على قدر عقولهم

ḫāṭibi l-nāsa ᶜalā qadri ᶜūqūlihim

Address the people according to their brains

Address people in the language they can understand

<u>201</u>

أخفض صوتك وقوي حجتك

ᵓaḫfiḍ ṣawtaka wa-qawwī ḥiğğataka

Lower your voice and strengthen your argument

<u>202</u>

أخف من الريشة

ᵓaḫaffu mina-l-rīšati

Lighter than a feather

<u>203</u>

إختلط حابلهم بنابلهم

ᵓiḫtalaṭa ḥābiluhum bi-nābilihim

The ropeman got mixed up with the archer

Applied to say that things got chaotic.

<u>204</u>

يخاف من خياله

yaḫāfu min ḫiyālihi

He is afraid of his own shadow

Said to describe a timid or a coward.

<u>205</u>

خوف الكلب ولا تضربه

ḫawwifi l-kalba wa-lā taḍribuhu

Scare the dog and do not hit it

<u>206</u>

إختر أهون الشرين

ʾiḫtar ʾahwana l-šarrayni

Choose the lesser of two evils

<u>207</u>

خير الأمور الوسط

ḫayru l-ʾumūri l-wasaṭu

The middle way is the best one

208

خير جليس في الزمان كتاب

ḫayru ǧalīsin fī l-zamāni kitābun

The best friend at all times is a book

209

خير الكلام ما قل ودل

ḫayru l-kalāmi mā qalla wa-dalla

The best words are those that were brief and guiding

Brevity is the soul of wit

210

خير الناس أحسنهم خلقا وأنفعهم للناس

ḫayru l-nāsi ᵓaḥsanuhum ḫilqan wa-ᵓanfaᶜuhum li-l-nāsi

The best of people are those with the best ethics and who are most useful to the people

211

الخير الوحيد في العالم هو المعرفة والشر الوحيد هو الجهل

al-ḫayru l-waḥīdu fī l-ᶜālami huwa l-maᶜrifatu
wa-l-šarru l-waḥīdu huwa l-ğahlu

The only good thing in the world is knowledge
and the only evil thing is ignorance

212

خيره لغيره

ḫayruhu li-ġayrihi

His good is passed to others

Applied to a man who is more generous to strangers than to himself or to his own family.

213

خيرها في غيرها

ḫayruhā fī ġayrihā

A better one in another one

Better luck next time

حرف الدال

The letter "dāl"

214

يدخل شعبان في رمضان

yudaḫḫilu Šaᶜbān fī Ramaḍān

He integrates the month of Sha'ban in the month of Ramadan, i.e. he mixes both lunar months together

Applied to a person who confuses the issues.

215

الدراهم بالدراهم تكسب

al-darāhimu bi-l-darāhimi tuksabu

Money with money is gained

Money makes money

216

دق الحديد وهو حام

diqqi l-ḥadīda wa-hwa ḥāmin

Strike while the iron is hot

217

دق على الخشب

diqq ᶜalā l-ḫašabi

Knock on wood

218

دلعوا الولد وربوه وإن كبر يعرف أمه وأباه

dalliᶜū l-walada wa-rabbūhu wa-ᵓin kabira yaᶜrifu ᵓummahu wa-ᵓabāhu

Spoil the child (with your affection) and educate him, so that when he grows up he knows his mother and father

219

الدم لا يصير ماءا

al-dammu lā yaṣīru māᵓan

Blood cannot turn into water

Applied to say that a bond with family/relatives can never break.

A house divided cannot stand

220

دمه ثقيل

dammuhu ṯaqīlun

His blood is heavy

Said about an unbearable person.

221

دوري في كل البلاد ولا تأخذي واحدا عنده أولاد

dawwirī fī kulli l-bilādi wa-lā taʾḫuḏī wāḥidan ʿindahu ʾawlādun

Wander (and look for a husband) in all the country and do not marry someone who has children

222

يدور على إبرة في كوم قش

yudawwiru ʿalā ʾibratin fī kawmi qaššin

He looks for a needle in a haystack

To find a needle in a haystack

223

الديك على مزبلته صياح

al-dīku ͨalā maḏbalatihi ṣayyāḥun

A cock crows best on his own dunghill

A dog is a lion when he is at home

224

الديك الفصيح من البيضة يصيح

al-dīku l-faṣīḥu mina l-bayḍati yaṣīḥu

An eloquent rooster crows from within its egg

It early pricks that will be a thorn

حرف الذال

The letter "ḏāl"

225

ذئب في ثوب حمل

ḏiʾbun fī ṯawbi ḥamalin

A wolf in sheep's clothing

Applied to say that appearances are not always what they seem to be.

An iron fist in a velvet glove

226

ذبح خروفين والضيوف إثنان

ḏabaḥa ḫarūfayni wa-l-ḍuyūfu ʾiṯnāni

He slaughtered two sheep and the guests were two

Said of a generous man.

227

ذهب الحمار يطلب قرنين فرجع مصلوم الأذنين

ḏahaba l-ḥimāru yaṭlubu qarnayni fa-rağiʿa maṣlūma l-ʾuḏunayni

The donkey went to ask for two horns and he returned with no ears

Applied to a greedy person who tries to get impossible things and who loses necessary things in the process.

228

أذل من الأرض

ʾaḏallu mina l-ʾarḍi

More vile or more submissive than the earth or ground

229

ذاق الأمرين

ḏāqa l-ʾamrayni

He tasted both (bitter) things

Applied to an unlucky person who falls from one bad situation into another.

<u>حرف الراء</u>

<u>The letter “rāʾ”</u>

<u>230</u>

رأسه كبير وعقله صغير

raʾsuhu kabīrun wa-ʿaqluhu ṣaġīrun

His head is big and his mind is small

Said of someone vain and narrow-minded.

<u>231</u>

أرى كل إنسان يرى عيب غيره ويعمى عن العيب الذي هو فيه

ʾarā kulla ʾinsāni yarā ʿayba ġayrihi wa-yuʿmā ʿani l-ʿaybi l-laḏī huwa fīhi

I see each person seeing the other person's defect and being blinded of his or her own defect

<u>232</u>

أرنا عرض كتفيك

ʾarinā ʿarḍa katifayka

Show us the width of your shoulders

Get lost!

233

رب أخ لك لم تلده أمك

Rubba ʾaḫin laka lam talidhu ʾummuka

You may have a brother that your mother didn't give birth to

Applied when you find a friend who cares for you like a brother would.

234

رب حرب شبت من لفظة

rubba ḥarbin šabbat min lafẓatin

More than one war has been enkindled by one word

235

رب ضارة نافعة

rubba ḍāratin nāfiʿatin

Many an afflicting matter has brought up something useful

Every delay has its blessing

Every cloud has a silver lining

The darkest hour is just before dawn

236

رب كلمة جلبت نقمة ورب كلمة جلبت نعمة

rubba kalimatin ğalabat naqmatan wa-rubba kalimatin ğalabat ni^{c}matan

Many a word uttered has brought ruin and many a word uttered has brought wealth

237

ربنا يبعث اللحم إلى الذي ليس له أسنان

rabbunā yab^{c}aṯu l-laḥma ^{ɔ}ilā l-laḏī laysa lahu ^{ɔ}asnānun

God sends meat to the one who does not have teeth

Applies to say that many are given opportunities that they cannot handle well due to a specific deficiency.

Good things come when we are too old to enjoy them

238

أربط الحصان عند الحمار أما يعلمه الشهيق وأما يعلمه النهيق

^{ɔ}irbiṭi l-ḥiṣāna ^{c}inda l-ḥimāri ^{ɔ}amma yu^{c}allimuhu l-šaḥīqa wa-ammā yu^{c}allimuhu l-nahīqa

Tether the horse near the donkey. Or he will teach him to bray with a hee or with a haw

Means that good persons with good manners can learn bad manners from bad persons.

He that lives with wolves will learn to howl

239

رزقه في رجليه

rizquhu fī riğlayhi

His livelihood is in his legs

Applied to someone who is better at making himself or herself look like a fool than being punished by criticizing others.

240

رجعت حليمة الى عادتها القديمة

rağiᶜat Ḥalīmat ᵓilā ᶜādatihā l-qadīmati

Halima returned to her old habit

Said of someone who keeps on doing the same habitual thing according to the same pattern.

Old habits die hard

241

رحلة الألف ميل تبدأ بالخطوة الأولى

riḥlatu l-ᵓalfi mīlin tabdaᵓu bi-l-ḫuṭwati l-ᵓūlā

The journey of a thousand miles begins with a single step

242

أرسل حكيما ولا توصيه

ᵓarsil ḥakīman wa-lā tuwassīhi

Send a wise man and do not advise him

Applies to say that a wise man knows the right thing to do.

243

إرضي بالقليل يأتيك الكثير

ᵓirḍī bi-l-qalīli yaᵓtīka l-kaṯīru

Be satisfied with little then much will come to you

Applied to a person who does not get satisfied unless getting a lot, though he or she will get more by learning to appreciate small things.

244

إرضاء الناس غاية لا تدرك

ʾirḍāʾu l-nāsi ġāyatun lā tudraku

Pleasing people is a matter that cannot be known

There's no contenting some people

245

الرفيق قبل الطريق

al-rafīqu qabla l-ṭarīqi

The friend is prior to the road

246

الرمد أهون من العمى

al-ramadu ʾahwanu mina-l-ʿamā

Trachoma is better than blindness

Meant to say that if the other option is the worst, then whatever you have is better than it.

Half a loaf is better than no bread

247

رمشة عين

ramšatu ʿaynin

In the blink of an eye

Applies to things that happen suddenly and quickly.

At the drop of a hat

248

إرم من وراء ظهرك

ʾirmi min warāʾi ẓahrika

Throw behind your back

Meaning to say do not care if there are false rumors going on about you.

249

إرميه في البحر يطلع وفي فمه سمكة

ʾirmīhi fī-l-baḥri yaṭlaʿu wa-fī famihi samakatun

Throw him in the sea, he will come up with a fish in his mouth

Said of a lucky person.

250

رهبوت خير من رحموت

rahabūtun ḫayrun min raḥamūtin

Fear is better than pity

Applied to say that it is better to be feared than pitied.

251

راح يخطب وتزوج

rāha yaḫṭubu wa-tazawwağa

He went to be engaged (to her) and married her

Applies to an agent who is sent for an arrangement and who takes advantage of the profit.

252

راحت الخيل لتنحدي مدت الخنفسة رجلها

rāḥati l-ḫaylu li-tanḥadī maddati l-ḫunfusatu riğluhā

(When) the horse went to get shoed, the beetle stretched out her leg

Applies to a person who makes himself or herself more important than what he is in reality.

253

راح يدور على الفائدة ورجع خسارته زائدة

rāḥa yudawwiru ᶜalā l-fāᵓidati wa-rağiᶜa ḫisāratuhu zāᵓidatun

He went looking for the profit and returned with a more increasing loss

254

راحت السكرة وجاءت الفكرة

rāḥati l-sakratu wa-ğāʾati l-fikratu

The drunkenness went away and the thinking came back

255

راح على حصان، رجع على بغل

rāḥa ᶜalā ḥiṣānin, rağaᶜa ᶜalā baġlin

He went on a horse and returned on a mule

Refers to a person who has a good position and great expectations and who returns with a loss.

256

راحت عليه

rāḥat ᶜalayhi

He missed the opportunity

257

إستراح من لا عقل له

ʾistarāḥa man lā ʿaqlun lahu

He found peace he who is without a mind

A fool lives in his own paradise

258

روحه طويل

rūḥuhu ṭawīlun

His soul is long

Said of a very patient person who endures a lot.

259

ريح في قفص

rīḥun fī qafaṣin

Like wind in a cage

Said of a fruitless action that has no effect.

260

يريد أن يعرف عن البيضة وعن من باضها

yurīdu ʾan yaʿrifa ʿani l-bayḍati wa-ʿan man bāḍaha

He wants to know about the egg and about who laid it

Is said about a very curious person.

<u>261</u>

تريد الحق ولا ابن عمه

turīdu l-ḥaqqa wa-lā bna ʿammihi

You want the truth and not its cousin

حرف الزال

The letter "zāl"

262

زوبعة في فنجان

zawba^catun fī finǧānin

A storm in a teacup

Applies to someone who makes a fuss about small things.

Tempest in a teapot

263

إزرع كل يوم تأكل

ʾizraʿ kullu yawmin taʾkulu

Plant each day and you shall eat

264

زمار الحي لا يطرب

zammāru l-ḥayyi lā yuṭribu

The village's piper does not exhilarate anyone

Meaning that the talents and accomplishments are highly regarded by everyone except by those at home.

A prophet is not without honor save in his own country

<u>265</u>

المتزوج اثنين واقع بين نارين

al-mutazawwiğu ᵓiṯnayna wāqiᶜun bayna nārayni

The one who is married with two (wives) has fallen between two fires

<u>266</u>

تزاوروا ولا تتجاوروا

tazāwarū wa-lā tatağāwarū

Visit each other but do not live close to each other

<u>267</u>

الزائد أخو الناقص

al-zāᵓidu ᵓaḫū l-nāqiṣi

The excessive is the brother of the incomplete

Moderation is best

Extremes meet

حرف السين

The letter "sīn"

268

أسـأله عن أبيه يقول لي هـارون أخوه

ʾasʾaluhu ʿan ʾabīhi yaqūlu lī Hārūna ʾaẖūhu

I ask him about his father, he tells me that Harun is his brother

Applied to a person who avoids answering a direct question by giving a different answer.

269

إسـأل مجربا ولا تسـأل حكيما

ʾisʾal muğarriban wa-lā tasʾal ḥakīman

Ask one who has experience (with the matter) and do not ask a physician

Experience without learning is better than learning without experience

270

ست وجاريتان على قلي بيضتين

sittun wa-ğāriyatāni ʿalā qalyi bayḍatayni

One lady and two maids occupied at frying two eggs

Said about using more of something than what is necessary.

A sledgehammer to crack a nut

271

سحب يده

saḥaba yadahu

He withdrew his hand

Refers to someone who does not want more to interfere or be involved in a matter.

To wash his hand of something

272

السرج المذهب لا يجعل الحمار حصانا

al-sarğu l-muḏahhabu lā yağᶜalu l-ḥimāra ḥiṣānan

The gilded saddle does not make the donkey a horse

All that glitters is not gold

273

أسرع من البرق

ʾasraʿu mina-l-barqi

Faster than lightning

274

يسرق الكحل من العين

yasruqu l-kuḥla mina l-ʿayni

He steals the mascara from the eye

Applied to describe someone who is very clever in deceiving others, for instance by persuading them to go against their best interests or by accepting something that is unnecessary.

He'd steal the shirt off your back

To sell ice to Eskimos

275

سرك أسيرك

sirruka ʾasīruka

Your secret is your prisoner

276

سرك في بئر

sirruka fī biʾrin

Your secret is in a well

Your secret is safe with me

277

سقط من عيني

saqaṭa min ʿaynī

He fell off my eye

Meaning I do not respect him anymore.

278

الساكت عن الحق شيطان أخرس

al-sākitu ʿani l-ḥaqqi šayṭānun ʾaḫrasun

He who is silent about the truth is a mute devil

279

السكوت علامة الرضا

al-sukūtu ʿalāmatu l-riḍā

Silence is the sign of approval

280

الإسكافي حاف وباب النجار مخلع

al-ʾiskāfī ḥāfin wa-bābu l-naǧāri muẖlaᶜun

The shoe-maker is barefooted and the carpenter's door is broken

The shoemaker's wife is always the worst shod

The shoemaker's son always goes barefoot

281

السلفة تربي العداوة

al-silfatu turabbī l-ᶜadāwata

Lending money engenders enmity

282

سلم عليه وعد اصابيعك

sallim ᶜalayhi wa-ᶜidd ʾaṣābīᶜaka

Shake hands with him and count your fingers afterwards

Refers to a dishonest person with whom one should be careful while dealing with.

Watch your back

283

سلام خادع شر من حرب مكشوف

salāmun ḫādiᶜun šarrun min ḥarbin makšūfin

A deceptive peace is worse than an open war

A bad peace is even worse than war

284

السلام على المعرفة

al-salāmu ᶜalā l-maᶜrifati

Greetings to knowledge

285

سلامة الإنسان في حلاوة اللسان

salāmatu l-ᵓinsāni fī ḥalāwati l-lisāni

The safety of a human is in the sweetness of his tongue

286

إسمع ولا تصدق

ᵓismaᶜ wa-lā tuṣaddiq

Listen and do not believe

Believe none of what you hear, and half of what you see

287

إستندت إلى خص مائل

ʾistanadtu ʾilā ḫaṣṣin māʾilin

I leant on a bent wall

I depended on someone who is not to be depended on.

288

سوء الخلق يعدي

sūʾu l-ḫuluqi yaʿdī

Bad manners contaminate

289

سود لي وجهي

sawwada lī waǧhī

He blackened my face

Applied to say that he made me feel awkward by his wrongdoing.

290

سال بهم السيل وجاش بنا البحر

sāla bihumu l-saylu wa-ǧāša bi-nā l-baḥru

The torrent flowed with them and the sea was unnavigable with us

Applied to say that they fell into a hard situation and we fell into one that is harder.

<u>حرف الشين</u>

<u>The letter "šīn"</u>

<u>291</u>

أشجع من ديك

ʾašǧaʿu min dīkin

More courageous than a cock

<u>292</u>

شحاد ومشارط

saḥḥādun wa-mušāriṭun

A beggar and he bargains!

Beggars cannot be choosers

<u>293</u>

أشد من الأرض

ʾăsaddu mina l-ʾarḍi

Harder than the earth or ground

<u>294</u>

شدة وتزول

šiddatun wa-tazūlu

A misfortune and it will pass

<u>295</u>

ينشرب مع الماء العكرة

yanšaribu ma^ca l-mā^ᵓi l-^cakirati

You could drink him with turbid water

Refers to someone who is very amiable.

<u>296</u>

يشرب من البئر ويرمي فيه حجرا

yašrabu mina l-biᵓri wa-yarmī fīhi ḥağaran

He drinks from the well and throws stones into it

Do not bite the hand that feeds you

<u>297</u>

شربة ماء

sirbatu māᵓin

A sip of water

A piece of cake

Easy to do

<u>298</u>

شرد من المطر ووقف تحت المرزاب

šarada mina l-maṭari wa-waqafa taḥta l-mirzābi

He moved away from the rain and stood under the gutter

Meant to say that he went from one bad situation into a worse one.

To jump out of the frying pan into the fire

<u>299</u>

الشراء خير من الاقتراض

al-širāʾu ḫayrun mina l-ʾiqtirāḍi

Better buy than borrow

<u>300</u>

انشغلوا ببيع السكن والميت لم يدفن بعد

ʾinšaġalū bi-bayʿi l-sakani wa-l-mayyitu lam yudfan baʿd

They got occupied in selling the house while the dead man did not get buried yet

301

شفيت نفسي ولكن جدعت أنفي

šafaytu nafsī wa-lākin ǧadaᶜtu ᵓanfī

I cured myself but I amputated my nose (in the process)

Applied when someone succeeds in doing something well but loses too much in the process.

302

أشكر من أنعم عليك وأنعم على من شكرك

ᵓuškur man ᵓanᶜama ᶜalayka wa-ᵓanᶜim ᶜalā man šakaraka

Thank the one who is generous to you and be generous to the one who thanks you

303

أشهر من راية البيطار

ᵓašharu min rāyati l-bayṭāri

More commonly known than the sign of the farrier

304

شائب يدللك ولا شاب يبهدلك

sāʾibun yudalliluki wa-lā šābun yubahdiluki

Better to have an old man who spoils you than a young man who disrespects you

حرف الصاد

The letter "ṣād"

305

يصب النار على الزيت

yaṣibbu l-nāra ᶜalā l-zayti

He adds fuel to the fire

To add fuel to the fire

306

صباح الخير يا جاري أنت بحالك وانا بحالي

ṣabāḥa l-ḫayri yā ğārī ᵓanta bi-ḥālika wa-ᵓanā bi-ḥālī

Good morning my neighbor. You mind your business and I mind my business

Good fences make good neighbors

307

الصبر يعين على كل عمل

al-ṣabru yuᶜīnu ᶜalā kulli ᶜamalin

Patience helps every work

308

الصبر مفتاح الفرج

al-ṣabru miftāḥu l-faraǧi

Patience is a remedy for every grief

309

صاحب الحق عينه قوية

ṣāḥibu l-ḥaqqi ᶜaynuhu qawiyyatun

The one with the right has a strong eye

Having a strong eye in the Arab world means to be bold and not to be worrying about what others say.

310

صاحب الدار أدرى بالذي فيه

ṣāḥibu l-dāri ᵓadrā bi-l-laḏī fīhi

The one who lives in the house knows best what is going on in it

311

صادق الثعالب وأبق فأسك جاهزا

ṣādiqi l-ṯaᶜāliba wa-ᵓabqī faᵓsaka ǧāhizan

Befriend the foxes but keep your axe ready

312

الصديق الصافي في وده لا تزعله ولا ترده

al-ṣadīqu l-ṣāfī fī waddihi la tuzᶜilhu wa-lā tariddhu

The friend who is pure in his affection, do not anger him or drive him away

313

الصديق وقت الضيق

al-ṣadīqu waqtu l-ḍīqi

A friend in need is a friend indeed

314

صديقك من أبكاك لا من أضحك

ṣadīkuka man ᵓabkāka lā man ᵓaḍḥakaka

Your friend is the one who made you cry not the one who made you laugh

315

أصعب شيء أن يعرف الانسان نفسه

ᵓaṣᶜabu šayᵓin ᵓan yaᶜrifa l-ᵓinsānu nafsahu

The most difficult thing is that the person knows himself or herself

316

صفر على الشمال

ṣifrun ᶜalā l-šimāli

A zero to the left

Applied to a worthless person, as the zero to the left of a number does not serve any purpose.

317

صف كلام

saffu kalāmin

A line of words

Empty talk

318

إصلاح الموجود خير من انتظار المفقود

ʾiṣlāḥu l-mawǧūdi ḫayrun mini ntiẓāri l-mafqūdi

Better to repair what is present than to wait for what is lost

Meaning be happy with what you have and don't long for something else.

319

الصانع السيئ يلوم أدواته

al-ṣāniᶜu l-sayyiᵓu yalūmu ᵓadawātahu

A bad workman blames his tools

A good workman does not quarrel with his tools

320

صنعة في اليد أمان من الفقر

ṣanᶜatun fī l-yadi ᵓamānun mina l-fiqri

A trade in hand insures against poverty

321

مصائب قوم عند قوم فوائد

maṣāᵓibu qawmin ᶜinda qawmin fawāᵓidun

The calamities of some people are benefits to some other people

One man's death is another man's breath

322

المصائب لا تأتي فرادى

al-maṣāᵓibu lā taᵓtī farādā

Disasters do not come one by one

323

الصيت الحسن خير من الغنى

al-ṣītu l-ḥasanu ḫayrun mina l-ġinā

A good name is better than riches

324

يتصيد في المياه العكرة

yataṣayyadu fī l-miyāhi l-ᶜakirati

He can fish in muddy water

Said of someone who seeks personal gains or rewards and is clever in seizing opportunities of a troubled or confused situation.

To fish in troubled waters

حرف الضاد

The letter "ḍād"

325

ضرب الحبيب زبيب

ḍarbu l-ḥabībi zabībun

The beloved one's hitting is as sweet as raisin

326

إضرب عصفورين بحجر

ʾiḍrib ʿuṣfūrayni bi-ḥağarin

Hit two birds with one stone

Kill two birds with one stone

327

إضرب ما دام الحديد حاميا

ʾiḍrib mā dāma l-ḥadīdu ḥāmiyun

Beat the iron while it is hot

328

ضربته والقبر

ḍarbatuhu wa-l-qabru

His hitting will put you in the grave

329

ضربني وبكى، سبقني و اشتكى

ḍarabanī wa-bakā, sabaqanī wa-štakā

He hit me and cried, he ran before me and complained (about me)

Applies to a person who insults someone else and yet believes to be the victim.

330

الضحك من غير سبب من قلة الأدب

al-ḍiḥku min ġayri sababin min qillati l-ʾadabi

Laughing for no reason is due to bad manners

The loud laugh bespeaks the vacant mind

331

أضيق الأمر أدناه من الفرج

ʾaḍyaqu l-ʾamri ʾadnāhu mina l-faraği

The harder the problem the closer it is to be solved

حرف الطاء

The letter "ṭāʾ"

332

طبقه

ṭabbaqahu

He convinced him

333

يطعم اللوز للذين ليس لهم أسنان

yuṭʿimu l-lawza li-l-laḏīna laysa lahum ʾasnānun

God feeds almonds to those without teeth

Good things sometimes come to those who do not deserve them

334

طق الحنك

ṭakku l-ḥanaki

Cracking the jaw

Refers to idle people talking senseless talk.

335

أطلب العلم ولو بالصين

ʾuṭlubu l-ʿilma wa-law bi-l-Ṣīn

Seek knowledge even in China

336

أطلبوا العلم من المهد إلى اللحد

ʾuṭlubū l-ʿilma mina l-mahdi ʾilā l-laḥdi

Seek knowledge from the cradle to the grave

337

طليقك لا ترديه وعشيقك لا تأخذيه

ṭalīquki lā taruddīhi wa-ʿašīquki lā taʾḫuḏīhi

Do not take back you ex-husband and do not marry your lover

338

طمعه قتله

ṭamaʿuhu qatalahu

His greed killed him

Gluttony kills more than the sword

339

طنجرة ولقيت غطاها

ṭanǧaratun wa-laqiyat ġaṭāhā

A pot that has found its lid

They both make a perfect match

Every Jack has a Jill

340

طنش

ṭannaša

He ignored it

Said of someone who does not want to pay attention to a matter.

341

طال الأبد على لبد

ṭāla l-ʾabadu ʿalā Lubad

The time became long to Lubad, the last, and the longest of life, of Lutmin's seven vultures

Applied to any thing that has been of long duration.

<u>342</u>

طار من الفرح

ṭāra mina l-faraḥi

He flew of happiness

<u>343</u>

الطيور على أشكالها تقع

ᵓal-ṭuyūru ᶜalā ᵓaškālihā taqaᶜu

Birds of the same kind flock together

Birds of a feather flock together

حرف الظاء

The letter "ẓāʾ"

344

ظل الكريم فسيح

ẓillu l-karīmi fasīhun

The shadow of the generous person is vast

Applied to say that a generous person can help a large number of people.

345

ظله ثقيل

ẓilluhu ṯaqīlun

His shadow is heavy

Said about an unbearable person.

346

ظلم الحكام وكيد النسوان وعناد الرهبان

ẓulmu l-ḥukkāmi wa-kaydu l-niswāni wa-ᶜinādu l-rahbāni

The oppression of rulers, the intrigue of women, and the obstinacy of monks (are things that are unbearable)

<u>347</u>

ظلم الأقارب أشد وقعا من السيف

ẓilmu l-ʾaqāribi āšaddu waqʿan mina-l-sayfi

The relatives' wrongdoing has a more harmful effect than the sword's

<u>348</u>

ظهره قوي

ẓahruhu qawiyyun

His back is strong

Said of someone who has a powerful position.

حرف العين

The letter "ᶜayn"

349

العتاب خير من الحقد

al-ᶜitābu ḫayrun mina-l-ḥiqdi

It is better to reproach than to hold a grudge

Better out than in

350

العجلة من الشيطان

al-ᶜağalatu mina-l-šayṭāni

Haste is the devil's work

Fools rush in

351

عدو يجاهرك العداء خير من صديق زائف

ᶜaduwwun yuğāhiruka l-ᶜadāᵓa ḫayrun min ṣadīqin zāᵓifin

Better an open enemy than a false friend

352

عدو عاقل خير من صديق جاهل

ᶜaduwwun ᶜāqilun ḫayrun min ṣadīqin ǧāhilin

Better to have a wise enemy than an ignorant friend

353

عداوة العاقل ولا صحبة الجاهل

ᶜadāwatu l-ᶜāqili wa-lā ṣiḥbatu l-ǧāhili

Better to have the enmity of the wise person than the friendship of the ignorant

354

عداوة الأقارب أوجع من لسع العقارب

ᶜadāwatu l-ᵓaqāribi ᵓawǧaᶜu min lasᶜati l-ᶜaqāribi

The relatives' enmity hurts more than the scorpions' sting

355

عذر البليد مسح السبورة

ᶜiḏru l-balīdi masḥu l-sabūrati

The excuse of the lazy moron is that he is cleaning the blackboard

356

عرج الجمل من شفته

ᶜaraǧa l-ǧamalu min šiffatihi

The camel limped from his split lip

Said of someone who sees problems outside of their contexts, for instance as having a little pain in the ear and taking it as an excuse not to walk.

357

إعرف صاحبك واتركه

ʾiᶜrif ṣāhibaka wa-trikhu

Know your friend and then leave him

358

يعرف الطير من تغريده والرجل من كلامه

yuᶜrafu l-ṭayru min taġrīdihi wa-l-raǧulu min kalāmihi

A bird is known by its singing and a man by his talk

359

عري قفاك للدبابير وقل يا رب أنت قدير

ᶜarrī qafāka li-l-dabābīri wa-qul yā rabba ᵓanta qadīrun

Expose your behind to the hornets and say: "Lord, You are mighty".

The meaning of the proverb is that one shouldn't complain at the consequences of one's own stupid actions.

360

أعز من الولد ولد الولد

ᵓaᶜazzu mina l-waladi waladu l-waladi

Only dearer than the child is the grand child

361

عاشر القوم أربعين يوماً. فإما صرت منهم وإما رحلت عنهم

ᶜāširi l-qawma ᵓarbaᶜīna yawman. fa-ᵓimma ṣirta minhum wa-īmma raḥalta ᶜanhum

Dwell among the people for forty days. You will either become one of them or you will leave them

<u>362</u>

تعاشروا كالإخوان وتحاسبوا كالغرباء

ta^cāšarū ka-l-ʾiḫwāni wa-taḥāsabū ka-l-ġurabāʾi

Frequent each other like brothers and make your accounts among each other like strangers

<u>363</u>

عصفور في اليد ولا عشرة على الشجرة

ᶜuṣfūrun fī l-yadi wa-lā ᶜašaratun ᶜalā l-šağarati

A bird in the hand and not ten on the tree

A bird in the hand is worth two on the bush

<u>364</u>

يعطي الحلق إلى الذي دون أذنين

yuᶜṭī l-ḥalaqa ʾilā l-laḏī dūna ʾuḏunayni

He (God) gives earrings to the one without ears

Applied to persons who are given opportunities that they cannot handle or do no deserve.

<u>365</u>

أعط الخبز لخبازه ولو أكل نصفه

ˀaᶜṭi l-ḫubza li-ḫubbāzihi wa-law ˀakala niṣfahu

Give the bread to its baker even if he eats half of it

Applies to say that it is better to give the job to an expert even if it will cost one more.

366

أعط كل ذي حق حقه

ˀaᶜti kulla ḏī ḥaqqin ḥaqqahu

Give each one who is entitled his due

Give the devil his due

367

أعطني حظا وارمني في البحر

ˀaᶜṭinī ḥaẓẓan wa-rminī fī-l-baḥri

Give me some good luck and throw me in the sea

368

أعطني صوفا وخذه خروفا

ˀaᶜṭinī ṣūfan wa-ḫuḏhu ḫarūfan

Give me wool and take it back as a sheep

Applies to say that you can profit from me.

369

عظمة الرجل تقاس بمدى استعداده للعفو على من أساء إليه

ᶜiẓmatu l-rağuli tuqāsu bi-madā stiᶜdādihi li-l-ᶜafwi ᶜalā man ᵓasāᵓa ᵓilayhi

The greatness of man is measured by his willingness to forgive those who wronged him

370

العظمة لله

al-ᶜiẓmatu li-l-lāhi

Only God is great

No one is perfect

371

عقربتان في حيط ولا بنتان في بيت

ᶜaqrabatāni fī ḥayṭin wa-lā bintāni fī baytin

Rather two scorpions on a wall than two girls in a home

372

العقل جوهرة

al-ᶜaqlu ğawharatun

The mind is a jewel

<u>373</u>

العقل السليم في الجسم السليم

al-ᶜaqlu l-salīmu fī l-ğismi l-salīmi

A sound mind in a sound body

<u>374</u>

عقلي ليس دفترا

ᶜaqlī laysa daftaran

My mind is not a notebook

Said when one forgets something important.

<u>375</u>

العلم بلا عمل كالشجر بلا ثمر

al-ᶜilmu bi-lā ᶜamalin ka-l-šağari bi-lā ṯamarin

Knowledge without work is like a tree without fruit

376

العلم والأدب خير من كنوز الفضة والذهب

al-ᶜilmu wa-l-ᵓadabu ḫayrun min kunūzi l-fiḍḍati wa-l-ḏahabi

Education and good manners are better than the treasures of silver and gold

377

علمي علمك

ᶜilmī ᶜilmuka

My knowledge is your knowledge

I know as much as you know

378

ستعلمك الأيام ما كنت تجهله

satuᶜallimuka l-ᵓayyāmu mā kunta tağhaluhu

Time will soon teach you what you were ignorant of

379

علمناهم الشحادة سبقونا على الأبواب

ᶜallamnāhum l-šaḥādata, sabaqūnā ᶜalā l-ʾabwābi

We taught them how to beg, they got before us to the doors

To beat someone at his own game

380

إعمل خيرا وارمه في البحر

ʾiᶜmil ḫayran wa-rmihi fī-l-baḥri

Do good and throw it in the sea

Don't expect rewards for a good deed

381

عامل الناس كا تحب أن يعاملوك

ᶜāmili l-nāsa kamā tuḥibbu ʾan yuᶜāmilūka

Treat the people like you want them to treat you

Do as you would be done

382

العمل يجعل الصعب سهلا

al-ᶜamalu yağᶜalu l-ṣaᶜba sahlan

Work renders what is difficult easy

383

العمل يقصر الأيام والبطالة تطولها

al-ᶜamalu yuqaṣṣiru l-ᵓayyāma wa-l-biṭālatu tuṭawwiluhā

Work shortens the days and unemployment lengthens them

384

الأعمال أعلى صوتا من الأقوال

al-ᵓaᶜmālu ᵓaᶜlā ṣawtan mina l-ᵓaqwāli

Actions speak louder than words

385

على رأس لساني

ᶜalā raᵓsi lisānī

It is on the tip of my tongue

Meaning that one is trying to remember something that one already knows.

386

على رأسي وعيني

ᶜalā raᵓsī wa-ᶜaynī

On my head and eyes

Applied to say that I'm at your service.

Your wish is my command

<u>387</u>

على قدر أهل العزم تأتي العزائم

ᶜalā qadri ᵓahli l-ᶜazmi taᵓtī l-ᶜazāᵓimu

Great gifts come from determined men

You can only go as far as you push

<u>388</u>

على قدر بساطك مد رجليك

ᶜalā qadri bisāṭika midd riğlayka

Stretch your legs as far as your carpet allows

Meant to say don't do what's beyond your capabilities or don't buy what you cannot afford.

Cut your coat according to your cloth

<u>389</u>

على قدر لحافك مد رجليك

ᶜalā qadri luḥāfika midd riğlayka

Stretch your legs as far as your quilt allows

This is a variant of the proverb above (388).

<u>390</u>

عمى العين ولا عمى القلب

ᶜamā l-ᶜayni wa-lā ᶜamā l-qalbi

The blindness of the eye is better than the blindness of the heart

<u>391</u>

عن المرء لا تسأل وسل عن قرينه

ᶜani l-marᵓi lā tasᵓalu wa-sal ᶜan qarīnihi

Don't ask of the man but ask about his companion

A man is known by the company he keeps

<u>392</u>

عند البطون ضاعت العقول

ᶜinda l-buṭūni ḍāᶜati l-ᶜuqūlu

When the stomachs are concerned, the minds went astray

Wisdom is overpowered by hunger

393

عند جهينة الخبر اليقين

ᶜinda Juhayna l-ẖabaru l-yaqīnu

The real truth is by Juhayna

Applied to say that no one knows the truth.

394

عند الشدائد تعرف الإخوان

ᶜinda l-šadāᵓidi taᶜrifu l-iẖwānu

Through adversities friends are known

Adversity tries friends

395

عند المضيق لا أخ ولا صديق

ᶜinda l-maḍīqi lā ᵓaẖun wa-lā ṣadīqun

At the narrow road, there is not a brother and nor a friend

In difficult situations one should think of saving oneself.

396

عند الامتحان يكرم المرء أو يهان

ᶜinda l-ˀimtiḥāni yukramu l-marˀu ˀaw yuhānu

By the examination, the person is honored or disgraced

A workman is known by his chips

The proof of the pudding is in the eating

397

عندما تغيب الهرة تلعب الفئران

ᶜindamā taġību l-hirratu talᶜabu l-fiˀrānu

When the cat is away the mice play

398

عنزة ولو طارت

ᶜanzatun wa-law ṭārat

It's a goat even if it flew

Said about an obstinate person who sticks to his or her statement no matter how foolish it is.

As stubborn as a mule

399

أعيث من جعار

ˀaᶜyaṯu min ǧaᶜārin

More mischievous than the she-hyena

400

تعالوا بمريضكم نطل عليه وتعالوا بميتكم نعزيه

ta^cālū bi-marīḍikum naṭullu ^calayhi wa-ta^cālū bi-mayyitikum nu^cazzīhi

Come with your sick one and we will watch over him, and come with your dead one and we will offer our condolences

Applied to lazy persons who want things coming to them.

401

عين لا ترى ولا قلب يحزن

^caynun lā tarā wa-lā qalbun yaḥzanu

What the eye does not see the heart does not grieve over

Meant to say that it is better not to be an eyewitness to misfortune as one will be saddened by it.

402

العين لا تعلو على الحاجب

al-^caynu lā ta^clū ^calā l-ḥāǧibi

The eye does not become higher than the eyebrow

Everyone should know his or her own position and respect the position of others.

حرف الغين

The letter "ġayn"

403

الغريق يتعلق بحبال الهواء

al-ġarīqu yataᶜallaqu bi-ḥibāli l-hawāᵓi

The drowning man hangs at the wind's ropes

In an emergency, desperate people will take any help from any source.

Any port in a storm

404

الغريق يتعلق بقشة

al-ġarīqu yataᶜallaqu bi-qaššatin

A drowning man clutches at a straw

Any port in a storm

405

الغزالة الشاطرة تغزل برجل حمار

al-ġazālatu l-šāṭiratu taġzilu bi-riğli ḥimārin

The clever deer can spin with the leg of a donkey

Applied to say that a skillful worker can do good work even with inadequate tools.

A good workman does not quarrel with his tools

<u>406</u>

إغسل وجهك لا تدري من سيقبله ونظف بيتك لا تدري من سيدخله

ʾiġsil waǧhaka lā tadrī man sayuqabbiluhu wa-naẓẓif baytaka lā tadrī man sayadḫuluhu

Wash you face for you do not know who will kiss it and clean your home for you do not know who will enter it

<u>407</u>

غضب المرأة كالحريقة ينطفئ في دقيقة

ġaḍabu l-marʾati ka-l-ḥarīqati yanṭafiʾu fī daqīqatin

The woman's anger is like fire, it extinguishes in a minute

<u>408</u>

غمض عينا وفتح عينا

ġammiḍ ᶜaynan wa-fattiḥ ᶜaynan

Close an eye and open an eye

Applies to say that things can happen very quickly.

In the blink of an eye

409

أغنى الأغنياء من لم يكن للبخل أسيرا

ᵓaġnā l-ᵓaġniyāᵓa man lam yakun li-l-buḫli ᵓasīran

The richest of men is the one who is not a prisoner of stinginess

410

الغني يا ما كثر اصحابه والفقير لا أحد يدق بابه

al-ġanīyu yā mā kaṯura ᵓaṣḥābuhu wa-l-faqīru lā ᵓahadun yaduqqu bābahu

The rich man, O how many friends he has, and the poor one no one knocks on his door

411

الغاية تبرر الوسيلة

al-ġāyatu tubarriru l-wasīlata

The end justifies the means

412

غابت السباع ولعبت الضباع

ġābati l-sibāᶜu wa-laᶜibati l-ḍibāᶜu

The lions were away and the hyenas played

When the cat is away, the mice will play

413

غيرة الجار ولا حسده

ġīratu l-ğāri wa-lā ḥasaduhu

It is better with the neighbor's jealousy than with his envy

<u>حرف الفاء</u>

<u>The letter “fāʾ”</u>

<u>414</u>

مفتاح الشر كلمة

miftāḥu l-šarri kalimatun

The key to evil is one word

<u>415</u>

الفجل إلى حد ما احمر لا يصير تفاحا

al-fiğlu ʾilā ḥaddi mā ḥmarra lā yaṣīru tuffāḥan

No matter how much the radish becomes red it does not become an apple

<u>416</u>

فرخ البط عوام

faraḫu l-baṭṭi ʿawwāmun

The son of a duck is a floater

Like father, like son

417

تفركش برماد سيكارة

tafarkaḫa bi-rimādi sīkāratin

He stumbled over a cigarette ash

Said about a person who has problems in performing his or her tasks or who makes a big fuss about a small injury.

418

الفزع يطير الوجع

al-fazaᶜu yuṭayyiru l-wağaᶜa

Fear drives pain away

419

فسر الماء بعد الجهد بالماء

fassara l-māᵓa baᶜda l-ğuhdi bi-l-māᵓi

After great effort, he explained the water with water

Applied to a person who does not know how to explain things.

420

يفصل قميصا للبرغوث

yufaṣṣilu qamīṣan li-l-barġūṯi

He makes a shirt for a flea

Applied to a person who is very meticulous.

421

الفضول قتل الهرة

al-fuḍūlu qatala l-hirrata

Curiosity killed the cat

422

الأفعال أبلغ من الأقوال

al-ʾafʿālu ʾablaġu mina l-ʾaqwāli

Actions speak louder than words

423

الفقير يرى البيضة بقرة

al-faqīru yarā l-bayḍata baqaratan

The poor man sees the egg as a cow

424

الفقير يقنع بقليله والبخيل لا يقنع بكثيره

al-faqīru yuqnaᶜu bi-qalīlihi wa-l-baẖīlu lā yuqnaᶜu bi-kaṯīrihi

The poor man is satisfied with the little he has and the stingy man is not satisfied with all the things he has

425

الفقير الذي ليس عليه دين غني

al-faqīru l-laḏī laysa ᶜalayhi daynun ġaniyyun

The poor man who has no debts is rich

426

فلاح ونزل إلى مدينة

fallāḥun wa-nazila ˀilā l-madīnati

A peasant and he is visiting the city

427

الفلوس تكسر النفوس تجعل العالي واطيا والسعيد متعوسا

al-fulūsu tukassiru l-nufūsa tağᶜalu l-ᶜāliya
wāṭiyan wa-l-saᶜīda matᶜūsan

Money breaks down the souls; it makes the
elevated person low and the happy one miserable

428

فوق الريح

fawqa l-rīḥi

On top of the wind

Said to describe a wealthy person or someone who is pleased with what he owns.

429

فوق كل طامة طامة

fawqa kulli ṭāmatin ṭāmatun

Above each calamity there is a calamity

One calamity after another

430

فمه ينقط عسل

famuhu yunaqqiṭu ᶜasalan

His mouth drips honey

A smooth talker

<u>431</u>

في التأني السلامة وفي العجلة الندامة

fī l-taʾanni l-salāmatu wa-fī l-ʿağalati l-nadāmatu

In caution there is safety; in haste repentance

<u>432</u>

في الحركة بركة

fī l-ḥarakati barakatun

There is a blessing in movement

Keep the pot boiling

<u>433</u>

في السوق ديوك وفي البيت ملوك

fī l-sūqi duyūkun wa-fī l-bayti mulūkun

At the market they are cocks and at home they are kings

Said to describe men who are not helpful.

حرف القاف

The letter "qāf"

434

قبل مرأتك تفرح حماتك

qabbil marʾataka tafraḥu ḥamātuka

Kiss your wife and your mother-in-law will be happy

435

قبل يد حماتك تحبك مرأتك

qabbil yada ḥamātika tuḥibbuka marʾatuka

Kiss your mother-in-law's hand and your wife will be happy

436

المستقبل كالمرأة الحامل لا أحد يعرف ماذا تنجب

al-mustaqbalu ka-l-marʾati l-ḥāmili lā ʾaḥadun yaʿrifu māḏā tanǧibu

The future is like the pregnant woman; no one knows what she will give birth to

437

يقتل القتيل ويمشي في جنازته

yaqtulu l-qatīla wa-yamšī fī ğināzatihi

He kills the victim and walks in his funeral

Applied for someone who stabs someone in the back then act as if he is innocent and sorry for him or her.

He hides like the snake in the grass

438

قد يجبن الشجاع بلا سلاح

qad yağbinu l-šuğāᶜu bi-lā silāḥin

The courageous might cower without a weapon

439

قدم السبت تلقى الأحد

qaddimi l-sabta talqā l-ᵓaḥada

Offer Saturday, you will find Sunday

Meant to say that when you do good things, they will come back to you. Also give and you'll get.

What goes around comes around

440

الأقربون أولى بالمعروف

al-ʾaqrabūna ʾawlā bi-l-maʿrūfi

The relatives are prior to be given assistance

Charity begins at home

441

القرد في عين أمه غزال

al-qirdu fī ʿayni ʾummihi ġazālun

The monkey in his mother's eyes is a gazelle

All her geese are swans

Beauty is in the eye of the beholder

442

المقروص من الثعبان يخاف من طرف الحبل

al-maqrūṣu mina -l-ṯaʿbāni yaḫāfu min ṭarafi l-ḥabli

He who is bitten by the snake is afraid of the end of the rope

The burnt child dreads the fire

443

أقصر من إبهام الضب

ᵓaqṣaru min ᵓibhāmi l-ḍabbi

Shorter than the great toe of the lizard

444

أقصر من إبهام الحبارى

ᵓaqṣaru min ᵓibhāmi l-ḥubārā

Shorter than the back toe of the bird called ḥubārā

445

أقصر من إبهام القطاة

ᵓaqṣaru min ᵓibhāmi l- qaṭāti

Shorter than the back toe of the bird called qaṭāti

446

قاضي الأولاد شنق حاله

qāḍī l-awlādi šanaqa ḥālahu

The children's judge hanged himself

<u>447</u>

قلب الاسطوانة

qalaba l-ʾisṭwānata

He turned the CD

Said of someone who changes the subject.

<u>448</u>

قلب المرء دليله

qalbu l-marʾi dalīluhu

A man's guide is his heart

To follow one's heart

<u>449</u>

قلب مليء بالحب دائما يهب الحب

qalbun malīʾun bi-l-ḥubbi dāʾiman yahibu l-ḥubba

A heart filled with love can always give love

<u>450</u>

قلبه أبيض

qalbuhu ʾabyaḍun

His heart is white

To have a heart of gold

<u>451</u>

إقلب الجرة على فمها تطلع البنت لأمها

ʾiqlibi l-ğarrata ʿalā famihā taṭlaʿu l-bintu li-ʾummihā

Turn the earthen pot upside down (on its mouth), the girl will still be like her mother

Like mother, like daughter

Like father like son

<u>452</u>

إنقلبت الآية

ʾinqalabati l-ʾāyatu

The verse was overturned

Said when someone's life situation is changed dramatically. Things have changed.

<u>453</u>

أقل الناس سرورا الحسود

ʾaqallu l-nāsa surūran al-ḥasūdu

The least happy among the people is the envious person

<u>454</u>

القناعة كنز لا يفنى

al-qanā^catu kanzun lā yufnā

Contentment is an inexhaustible treasure

<u>455</u>

قالوا للبغل من أبوك قال الفرس خالي

qālū li-l-baġli man ᵓabūka, qāla al-ḥiṣānu ḫālī

They said to the mule: "Who is your father?". He said: "The horse is my maternal uncle".

Applied to someone of low origin but who boasts of some distant aristocratic kin.

<u>456</u>

نقول له: ثور يقول أحلبه

naqūlu lahu: ṯawrun, yaqūlu ᵓaḥlibuhu

We tell him: "it's a bull", he says: "I'll milk it".

Said about a stupid man with whom there is no use advising.

457

قل الحق ولو كان مرا

quli l-ḥaqqa wa-law kāna murran

Say the truth even if it was bitter

458

قام الدب ليرقص، قتل سبعة ثمانية انفس

qāma l-dibbu li-yarqusa, qatala sabᶜata ṯamāniyata ᵓanfusin

The bear got up to dance and killed seven eight persons

Is said about a very clumsy person.

459

قيمة كل امرئ ما يحسنه

qīmatu kulli mraᵓin mā yuḥsinuhu

The worth of each man consists in what he does well

<u>حرف الكاف</u>

<u>The letter "kāf"</u>

<u>460</u>

كأم العروس

ka-ᵓummi l-ᶜarūsi

Like the mother of the bride

Applied to a person who pretends to be very busy just to attract attention.

As busy as a hen with one chicken

<u>461</u>

كأنه بالع راديو

ka-ᵓannahu bāliᶜun rādiū

It is as though he swallowed a radio

Refers to someone who talks too much.

<u>462</u>

كأنه ماش على قشور بيض

kaᵓannahu māšin ᶜalā qušūri bayḍin

As though he were walking on eggshells

Applies to a person who is afraid of upsetting someone. He or she takes very cautious, quiet and gentle steps.

463

كبائع الماء في حي السقاة

ka-bā'i'i l-mā'i fī ḥayyi l-suqāti

Like the seller of water in the quarter of the water carriers

Applied to a person who is doing a fruitless deed or is selling a product that does not sell.

Carrying water to Venice

To carry coals to Newcastle

464

كحكم قراقوش

ka-ḥikmi Qarāqūš

Like the ruling of Qaraqūš

Qaraqūš was a Mamlūk ruler who ruled without any logical basis. Applies to a person who imposes illogical rules and demands.

<u>465</u>

كالسمن على العسل

ka-l-samani ᶜalā l-ᶜasali

Like the butter on the honey

Said of two people who are compatible and perfect for each other.

<u>466</u>

كالشمعه تحرق نفسها كي تنور للناس

ka-l-šamᶜati taḥriqu nafsahā kay tunawwira li-l-nāsi

Like the candle it burns itself out to give light to the people

Applied to a generous person.

<u>467</u>

أكبر منك بيوم أعرف منك بسنة

ʾakbaru minka bi-yawmin ʾaᶜrafu minka bi-sanatin

Older than you by a day, more knowledgeable than you by a year

468

المكتوب يعرف من عنوانه

al-maktūbu yu^crafu min ^cinwānihi

The letter is known by the address on the envelope

An ass is know by his ears

469

كثير الكارات قليل البارات

kaṯīru l-kārāti qalīlu l-bārāti

A rolling stone gathers no moss

Refers to a person who keeps on moving and thus avoids attending his or her responsibilities.

470

كثرة الطباخين تفسد الطبيخ

kiṯratu l-ṭabbāḫīna tafsidu l-ṭabīḫa

Too many cooks spoil the broth

471

كثرة العتاب تفرق الأحباب

kiṯratu l-^citābi tufarriqu l-^ɔaḥbāba

Too much reproach separates loving persons from each other

<u>472</u>

التكرار يعلم الحمار

al-tikrāru yu^callimu l-ḥimāra

Repetition teaches the donkey

Practice makes perfect

<u>473</u>

كسر حجارا ولا تلعب قمارا

kassir ḥiğāran wa-lā tal^cabu qimāran

Break stones but do not play poker

<u>474</u>

الكسلان لا يمشي في الشمس لكي لا يجرجر ظله وراءه

al-kaslānu lā yamšī fī l-šamsi li-kay lā yuğarğiru ẓillahu warā^ɔahu

The lazy one does not walk in the sun so he does not drag his shadow behind him

475

كل ابن آدم خطاء

kullu bni ᵓādami ḫaṭṭāᵓun

Every human being errs

To err is human

476

كل تأخيرة فيها خيرة

kullu taᵓḫīratin fīhā ḫayratun

Every delay has its blessing

Every cloud has a silver lining

477

كل رأس به صداع

kullu raᵓsin bihi ṣudāᶜun

Every head has a headache

478

كل خرابة ولنا فيها عفريت

kullu ḫarābatin wa-lanā fīhā ᶜifrītun

In every ruin we find a devil

Applied to say that wherever we go we find someone to ruin our plans.

479

كل سر جاوز الإثنين شا ع

kullu sirrin ğāwaza l-ᵓiṯnayna šāᶜa

Every secret that was shared between more than two persons spread

A secret between more than two is no secret

480

كل شيء اذا كثر رخص إلا الأدب

kullu šayᵓin ᵓiḏā kaṯura raḫiṣa ᵓillā l-ᵓadabu

Everything if it became much becomes cheap except ethics

481

كل الطرق تؤدي إلى روما

kullu l-ṭuruqi tuᵓaddī ᵓilā Rūmā

All roads take to Rome

482

كل طلعة وراءها نزلة

kullu ṭal^c atin warā^ʾ hā nazlatun

Every rise has after it a fall

Every tide has its ebb

483

كل عقدة لها حلال

kullu ^c iqdatin lahā ḥallālun

Every knot has someone to undo it

484

كل ما يعجبك والبس ما يعجب الناس

kul mā yu^c ğibuka wa-lbis mā yu^c ğibu l-nāsa

Eat whatever you like and dress in whatever people admire

485

كل ممنوع مرغوب

kullu mamnū^c in marġūbun

Everything that is forbidden is desired

Forbidden fruit is the sweetest

Stolen kisses are sweet

486

كل واحد له قادح ومادح

kullu wāḥidin lahu qādiḥun wa-mādiḥun

Everyone has a detractor and an adulator

487

الكلب الحي افضل من الأسد الميت

al-kalbu l-ḥayyu ʾafḍalu mina l-asadi l-mayyiti

A living dog is better than a dead lion

488

كلب الشيخ شيخ

kalbu l-šayḫi šayḫun

The dog of the Sheik is a Sheik

Like master like man

489

الكلاب تنبح والقافلة تسير

al-kilābu tanbaḥu wa-l-qāfilatu tasīru

The dogs bark but the caravan moves on

490

الكلاب النابحة نادرا ما تـعض

al-kilābu l-nābiḥatu nādiran mā taᶜaḍḍu

Barking dogs seldom bite

Applied to say that those who make loud threats seldom carry them out.

491

أكلمك يا بنتي وأسمعك يا كنتي

ᵓukallimuki yā bintī wa-ᵓusammiᶜuki yā kinnatī

I speak to you, my daughter, I let you hear, my daughter-in-law

Refers to making remarks and giving hints to a person indirectly by talking to another. Also beating someone to threaten someone else.

492

تكلم فقد كلم الله موسى

takallam fa-qad kallama l-lāhu Mūsā

Speak, for God spoke to Moses
Applied to say that even superiors talk to inferiors.

493

تكلمه لا يسمع وترسله لا يرجع

tukallimuhu lā yasmaᶜu wa-tursiluhu lā yarǧaᶜu

You talk to him he does not listen, you send him (to do something) he does not come back

494

كلمة الحق تجرح

kalimatu l-ḥaqqi taǧraḥu

The word of truth hurts

The truth hurts

495

كلمة تحنن وكلمة تجنن

kalimatun tuḥanninu wa-kalimatun tuǧanninu

One word makes one tender and one word makes one mad

496

الكلمة الطيبة تجد مكانا في كل قلب

al-kalimatu l-ṭayyibatu tağidu makānan fī kulli qalbin

The kind word finds a place in every heart

497

كلام البغيض يغيظ

kalāmu l-baġīḍi yuġīẓu

The hateful person's words irritate

498

كلام يجر كلاما

kalāmun yağurru kalāman

One talk drags another talk

Said of someone who goes on talking.

499

كم علمته نظم القوافي فلما قال قافية هجاني

kam ᶜallamtuhu naẓma l-qawāfī wa-lammā qāla qāfiyatan hağānī

How much did I teach him how to write rhymes
and when he recited a rhyme he satirized me

Ingratitude is the world's reward

<u>500</u>

كان هذا في آباد الدهر

kāna hāḏā fī ʾābādi l-dahri

This was a long time ago

<u>501</u>

تكون جمرة وستصير رمادا

takūnu ǧamratan wa-sataṣīru rimādan

It may be a fire and it shall be ashes

Meant to say that violent passions easily subside.

<u>502</u>

كن على حذر فالدنيا دار رحيل

kun ʿalā ḥaḏirin fa-l-dunyā dāru raḥīlin

Be careful for the world is a place of departure

حرف اللام

The letter "lām"

503

لأجل الورد أسقيك يا عليق

li-ʾağli l-wardi ʾasqīka yā ʿalliqu

For the sake of the flowers, I water you, O weeds

Applies to situations when one has to nourish a few relations for the sake of being close to someone one loves.

504

لتقل خيرا أو لتصمت

li-taqul ḫayran ʾaw li-taṣmit

Or you say good things or you're silent

Better be silent than speak ill

505

لكل بداية نهاية

li-kulli bidāyatin nihāyatun

For every beginning there is an end

506

لكل جديد بهجته

li-kulli ǧadīdin bahǧatuhu

Everything new has its joy

New brooms sweep clean

507

لكل جديد لذة

li-kulli ǧadīdin liḏḏatun

Novelty gives pleasure

508

لكل جواد كبوة ولكل عالم هفوة

li-kulli ǧawwadin kabwatun wa-li-kulli ᶜālimin hafwatun

Any horse may stumble, any sage may err

Meant to say that everyone has his or her faults.

Homer sometimes nods, and this is a good horse that never stumbles

509

لكل مقام مقال ولكل زمان رجال

li-kulli maqāmin maqālun wa-li-kulli zamānin riğālun

Every place has its words to be said and every time has its men

510

للضرورة أحكام

li-l-ḍurūrati ᵓaḥkāmun

Necessity has its own laws

Necessity knows no law

511

للناس في ما يعشقون مذاهب

li-l-nāsi fī mā yaᶜšiqūna maḏāhibun

People have different doctrines concerning the objects of their love

Tastes and colors are not argued over

512

لا أحد يعرف حالك إلا الله ثم جارك

lā ᵓaḥad yaᶜrifu ḥālaka ᵓillā l-lāhu ṯumma ğāruka

No one knows about your situation except God and then your neighbor

<u>513</u>

لا تؤخر عملك إلى الغد ما تقدر أن تعمله اليوم

*lā tu*ʾ*aḫḫiru* ᶜ*amalaka* ʾ*ilā l-ġadi mā taqdiru* ʾ*an ta*ᶜ*malahu l-yawma*

Do not postpone your work to tomorrow what you can do today

<u>514</u>

لا تأكل خبزك على مائدة غيرك

*lā ta*ʾ*kulu ḫubzaka* ᶜ*alā mā*ʾ*idati ġayrika*

Don't eat your bread on someone else's table

<u>515</u>

لا تبع فروة الدب قبل صيده

*lā tabi*ᶜ *farwata l-dibb qabla ṣaydihi*

Don't sell the skin of the bear before you've killed it

Don't count your chickens before they are hatched

516

لا يجمع سيفان في غمد

lā yuğma^cu sayfāni fī ġamadin

Two swords do not fit in one sheath

A man cannot serve two masters

517

لا تحتقر مسكينا وكن له معينا

lā taḥtaqiru miskīnan wa-kun lahu mu^cīnan

Do not despise a poor man but be helpful to him

518

لا تحكم على الحصان من سرجه

lā taḥkumu ^calā l-ḥiṣāni min sarğihi

Judge not the horse by its saddle

519

لا يحمل همك إلا الذي من دمك

lā yaḥmilu hammaka ^ɔillā l-laḏī min dammika

No one carries your worries unless the one who has the same blood as you

520

لا يرضى عنك الحسود حتى تموت

lā yarḍā ᶜanka l-ḥasūdu ḥattā tamūta

The envious will not be pleased with you until you die

521

لا تسقط من كفه خردلة

lā tasquṭu min kaffihi ḫardalatun

He does not drop a mustard

522

لا تصدق كل ما تسمع ونصف ما ترى

lā tuṣaddiq kulla mā tasmaᶜu wa-niṣfa mā tarā

Believe none of what you hear, and half of what you see

523

لا صداقة الا بعد عداوة

lā ṣadāqatun ᵓillā baᶜda ᶜadāwatin

There is no friendship unless after an enmity

524

لا يعجبه العجب

Lā yu^{c}ğibuhu l-^{c}ağaba

He is not (even) impressed by a wonder

Applies to a person who is very difficult in being pleased.

525

لا يعرف التمرة من الجمرة

lā ya^{c}rifu l-tamrata mina l-ğamrati

He does not know the date from the ember

Said about a stupid man who cannot differentiate between different things.

526

لا يعرف قيمة الشيء إلا صاحبه

lā ya^{c}rifu qīmata l-šay$^{\circ}$i $^{\circ}$illā ṣāḥibuhu

Only the one who owns the thing knows its value

527

لا يعرف كوعه من بوعه

lā ya^{c}rifu kū^{c}ahu min bū^{c}ihi

He does not know his elbow from his mouth

This is a variant of the proverb above (519).

528

لا يتعلم الإنسان إلا من كيسه

lā yataᶜallamu l-ᵓinsānu ᵓillā min kīsihi

The human being does not learn anything unless from his own bag

529

لا تعاند من إذا قال فعل

lā tuᶜānidu man ᵓiḏā qāla faᶜala

Do not fight the man who does what he says

530

لا غريب إلا الشيطان

lā ġarībun ᵓillā l-šayṭānu

There is no stranger unless Satan

531

لا يكابر في الامور إلا غبي أو مغرور

lā yukābiru fī l-ʾumūri ʾillā ġabiyyun ʾaw maġrūrun

Only a stupid or an arrogant man turns matters into controversies

532

لا كرامة لنبي في وطنه

lā karāmatun li-nabiyyin fī waṭanihi

The prophet has no honor in his country

A prophet is not without honor save in his own country

533

لا تلعب معه

lā talʿab maʿahu

Don't mess with him

534

لا يستمتع بالجوزة إلا كاسرها

lā yastamtiʿu bi-l-ǧawzati ʾillā kāsiruhā

Only he who breaks the nut enjoys it

535

لا يمكن حمل بطيختين بيد واحدة

lā yumkinu ḥamlu baṭṭīḫatayni bi-yadin wāḥidatin

One cannot carry two melons in one hand

A man cannot serve two masters

536

لا تنام بين القبور ولا ترى منامات وحشة

lā tanām bayna l-qubūri wa-lā tarā manāmātin waḥšatan

Do not sleep among the graves and you will not see nightmares

537

لا يوجد أحد كامل

lā yūǧadu ʾaḥadun kāmilun

There is no one who is perfect

No one is perfect

538

لا يوجد أي جديد تحت الشمس

lā yūğadu ᵓayyu ğadīdin taḥta l-šamsi

There is nothing new under the sun

539

لا يوجد دخان بلا نار

lā yūğadu duḫḫānun bi-lā nārin

There is no smoke without fire

540

لا يوجد رسول كالدرهم

lā yūğadu rasūlun ka-l-dirhami

There is no prophet like money

Money talks, bullshit walks

541

لا يوجد مصيبة أعظم من الجهل

lā yūğadu muṣībatun ᵓaᶜẓamu mina l-ğahli

There is not a calamity greater than ignorance

542

لا يوجد نتيجة بدون ألم، لا حلاوة بدون نار

lā yūǧadu natīǧatun bi-dūni ʾalamin,
lā ḥalāwatun bi-dūni nārin

There is no result without pain, no pleasure without fire

No gains without pains

<u>543</u>

لا يقع الثعلب مرتين في نفس الفخ

lā yaqaᶜu l-ṯaᶜlabu marratayni fī nafsi l-faḫḫi

The fox is not taken twice in the same snare

<u>544</u>

لا تكن صلبا فتكسر ولا لينا فتعصر

lā takun ṣalban fa-tuksaru wa-lā layyinan fa-tuᶜṣaru

Do not be too hard, lest you will be broken; do not be too soft, lest you will be squeezed

<u>545</u>

الذي يأتي بسهولة يذهب بسهولة، ما لا تجلبه الرياح تأخذه الزوابع

al-laḏī yaʾtī bi-suhūlatin yaḏhabu bi-suhūlatin,
mā lā taǧlibuhu l-riyāhu taʾḫuḏuhu l-zawābiᶜu

What comes easily goes easily, what the wind does no carry away the storm takes

Easy come, easy go

546

الذي يأكل على ضرسه ينفع نفسه

al-la<u>d</u>ī ya^ɔkulu ^calā ḍirsihi yanfa^cu nafsahu

The one who chews with his own teeth benefits himself

God helps those who help themselves

547

الذي باعك ببصلة، بعه بقشرتها

al-la<u>d</u>ī bā^caka bi-baṣlatin, bi^chu bi-qišratihā

He who sold you for an onion, sell him for its shell

548

الذي تحسبه موسى يكون فرعونا

al-la<u>d</u>ī taḥsibuhu Mūsā yakūnu Far^cūnā

The one you think is Moses turns out to be Pharaoh

Applied when one is misjudging people. The one you think is nice is not.

A wolf in a sheep's clothing

An iron fist in a velvet glove

549

الذي يحلف كثيرا يكذب كثيرا

al-laḏī yaḥlifu kaṯīran yakḏibu kaṯīran

He who swears a lot lies a lot

550

الذي تخفيه الليالي تظهره الأيام

al-laḏī tuḫfīhi l-layālī tuẓhiruhu l-ʾayyamu

What the nights conceal the days will show

551

الذي يخاف من العفريت يظهر له

al-laḏī yaḫāfu mina l-ʿifrīti yaẓhuru lahu

The one who is afraid of the demon will have him appearing to him

552

الذي يتزوج أمي أقول له عمي

al-lad̲ī yataǧawwazu ᵓummī ᵓaqūlu lahu ᶜammī

He who marries my mother, I call him my uncle

Meant to say that if you can't beat them, join them.

553

الذي يسرق البيضة يسرق الجمل

al-laḍī yasruqu l-bayḍata yasruqu l-ǧamala

He who steals the egg steals the camel

Applied to say that a small theft is as bad as a major one.

He who steals an egg will steal an ox

554

الذي يعطي لابنه سمكة يطعمه في يومه والذي يعلم ابنه صيد السمك يطعمه طول الأيام

al-lad̲ī yuᶜṭī li-bnihi samakatan yuṭᶜimuhu fī yawmihi wa-l-lad̲ī yuᶜallimu bnahu ṣayda l-samaki yuṭᶜimuhu ṭūla l-ᵓayyāmi

He who gives a fish to his son feeds him for one day, he who teaches his son how to fish feeds him for all days

555

الذي علينا عملناه والباقي على الله

al-la<u>d</u>ī ᶜalaynā ᶜamilnāhu wa-l-bāqī ᶜalā l-lāhi

What we had to do we did it and the rest is up to God

556

الذي يعوز الكلب يقول له صباح الخير يا سيدي

al-la<u>d</u>ī yaᶜūẓu l-kalba yaqūlu lahu ṣabāḥa l-ḫayri ya sayyidī

He who needs (something from) the dog tells him: "Good morning, milord"

557

الذي عينك عليه عين غيرك عليه

al-la<u>d</u>ī ᶜaynuka ᶜalayhi ᵓaynu ġayrika ᶜalayhi

Whatever you find attractive, others find attractive too

Meant to say that if one does not get what one desires when one has the opportunity to get it, then others will get it.

No time like the present

558

الذي فات مات

al-laḏī fāta māta

What has happened in the past has died

Let bygones be bygones

559

الذي مكتوب على الجبين يجب أن تراه العين

al-laḏī maktūbun ᶜalā l-ğabīni yağibu ᵓan tarāhu l-ᶜaynu

What is written on the forehead, the eye must see

What must be, must be

560

الذي لا يشبع من بيته لا يشبع من بيت الجيران

al-laḏī lā yašbaᶜu min baytihi lā yašbaᶜu min bayti l-ğīrāni

He who does not get satiated from his own home will not get satiated from the neighbors' home

561

الذي لا يطول لقطف العنب بقول أنها حامضة

al-laḏī lā yaṭūlu li-qaṭfi l-ᶜinabi yaqūlu ᵓannahā ḥamiḍatun

The one who does not reach to pick up the grapes says that they are sour

When the fox cannot reach the grapes he says they are not ripe

When the monkey can't reach the ripe banana, he says it is not sweet

562

الذي لا يعرف أن يرقص يقول بأن الأرض عوجاء

al-laḏī lā yaᶜrifu ᵓan yarqusa yaqūlu bi-ᵓanna l-ᵓarḍa ᶜawǧāᵓun

He who does not know how to dance says that the ground is crooked

563

الذي لا يعرف الصقر يشويه

al-laḏī lā yaᶜrifu l-saqra yašwīhi

He who does not know the falcon grills it

Applied to say that regrettable deeds are performed through ignorance. He who does not know the nature of things finds everything similar. He who cannot differentiate between different persons cannot know the value of one person. Also said about people who mistreat other people due to their ignorance.

564

الذي لا يقع لا يقوم

al-laḏī lā yaq̌aᶜu lā yaqūmu

He who doesn't fall, doesn't get up

565

الذي له رجله في الماء ليس كالذي له رجله في النار

al-laḍī lahu riğluhu fī l-māᵓi laysa ka-l-laḍī lahu riğluhu fī-l-nāri

He who has his foot in the water is not like the one who has his foot in the fire

Meant to say that attitudes are formed by circumstances.

566

الذي يمد رجليه لا يمد يديه

al-laḏī yamuddu riğlayhi lā yamuddu yadayhi

He who stretches his legs should not stretch his hands

Applied to a needy man who is haughty and gives himself airs.

567

الذي يمدح نفسه كذاب

al-laḏī yamdaḥu nafsahu kaḏḏābun

He who praises himself is a liar

Self-praise is no recommendation

568

الذي يمشي وراء الديك يوديه إلى الدمنة

al-laḏī yamšī warāʾa l-dīki yuwaddīhi ʾilā l-dumnati

He who follows the cock is sent by him to the barn

Means to say that he or she who follows a stupid or evil person is sent to his or her destruction.

569

الذي ينظر إلى فوق تنكسر رقبته

al-laḏī yanẓuru ʾilā fawqin tankasiru raqbatuhu

He who looks up too much can have his neck broken

Is meant to say that a person who envies others will suffer.

He who looks up too much gets a pain in the neck

He that gazes upon the sun shall at last be blind

570

الذي يكبر فشخته يقع

al-laḏī yukabbiru fašḫtahu yaqaᶜu

He who over-lengthens his step will fall

571

اللسان عدو الانسان

al-lisānu ᶜaduwwu l-ᵓinsāni

The tongue is the person's enemy

572

اللسان مفتاح الخير والشر

al-lisānu miftāhu l-ḫayri wa-l-šarri

The tongue is the key of good and evil

573

لسانك حصانك إن صنته صانك وإن هنته هانك

lisānuka ḥiṣānuka ʾin ṣintahu ṣānaka, wa-ʾin hintahu hānaka

Your tongue is your horse — if you take care of it, it takes care of you; if you betray it, it will betray you

574

اللقم تمنع النقم

al-liqamu tamnaʿu l-naqama

Food bites prevent curses

575

الله يخرجنا من دار العيب بلا عيب

al-lāhu yuḫriğunā min dāri l-ʿaybi bi-lā ʿaybin

May God pull us out from the house of disgrace without any shortcomings

576

الله يرزق صاحبي كي يعطيني

al-lāhu yurziqu ṣadīqī kay ya^cṭiyanī

May God make my friend wealthy so that he will give me (of his wealth)

577

الله يعين الرجل االذي يقع بين يدين المرأة ولسانها

al-lāhu yu^cīnu l-rağula l-laḏī yaqa^cu bayna yadayni l-mar^cati wa-lisānihā

May God help the man who falls victim to the woman's manipulation and her tongue

578

لم يطل توت الشام ولا عنب اليمن

lam yaṭil tūta l-Šāmi wa-lā ^cinaba l-Yamani

He did not reach nor the berries of Damascus nor the grapes of Yemen

Said about a greedy person who went on an expedition and returned empty handed.

579

لم ينقل أخبارك إلا من دخل دارك

lam yanqul ᵓaḫbāraka ᵓilla man daḫala dāraka

Only the one who enters your home sends out news about you

580

إلهي الكلب بعظمة

ᵓilhī l-kalba bi-ᶜaẓmatin

Distract the dog with a bone

581

لم يحك ظهري مثل يدي

lam yaḥukk ẓahrī miṯla yadī

Nothing scratches my back (better) than my hand

Meaning that one should abstain from relying on others.

582

لم يلقوا عيبا في الورد وقالوا له يا أحمر الخدين

lam yalqū ᶜayban fī l-wardi fa-qālū lahu yā ᵓaḥmara l-ḫaddayni

They did not find any flaw in the flower, so they said to it: "O you, with the too red cheeks".

Applied to someone who tries to find flaws in everything.

<u>583</u>

لما كنت لحمة أكلوني ولما صرت عظمة رموني

lammā kuntu laḥmatan ᵓakalūnī wa-lammā ṣirtu ᶜaẓmatan ramūnī

When I was a meat they ate me, and when I became a bone they threw me

<u>584</u>

لما الهرم يتحرك

lammā l-haramu yataḥarraku

When the Pyramid moves

Applied when one means that an event will never happen.

When pigs fly

When the cows come home

<u>585</u>

لن ترجع الأيام التي مضت

lan tarǧaᶜa l-ᵓayyāmu l-latī maḍat

The days that have passed will not return

586

لن تعرف خيري حتى تجرب غيري

lan taᶜrifa ḫayrī ḥattā tuğariba ġayrī

You wouldn't know how good I am until you try someone else

587

لو فيه خير لم يرمه الطير

law fīhi ḫayrun lam yarmihi l-ṭayru

If it or he was of any use the bird would not have thrown it or him away

588

لو كانت السماء تستجيب لدعاء الكلاب لأمطرت عظاما

law kānati l-samāᵓu tastağību li-duᶜāᵓi l-kilābi la-ᵓamṭarat ᶜiẓāman

If the sky listened to the prayer of the dogs it would let bones rain

If wishes were horses, beggars would ride

589

لولا العلم لكان الناس كالبهائم

law lā l-ᶜilmu la-kāna l-nāsu ka-l-bahāʾimi

Had it not been for knowledge the people would be like animals

590

ليس الجمال بأثواب تزيننا إن الجمال جمال العلم والأدب

laysa l-ǧamālu bi-ʾaṯwābin tuzayyinunā, ʾinna l-ǧamāla ǧamālu l-ᶜilmi wa-l-ʾadabi

Beauty is not in the clothes that decorate us; beauty is in the beauty of science and ethics

591

ليس العيب لمن كان فقيرا بل العيب لمن كان بخيلا

laysa l-ᶜaybu li-man kāna faqīran bali l-ᶜaybu li-man kāna baḫīlan

The flaw is not on he who is poor but the flaw is on he who is stingy

592

ليس العار أن نقع ولكن العار أن لا نستطيع النهوض

laysa l-ᶜāru ᵓan naqaᶜa wa-lakinna l-ᶜāra ᵓan lā nastaṭīᶜu l-nuhūḍa

There is no shame in falling, but there is a shame if we are unable to get up

593

ليس كل الحجارة توافق للعمارة

laysa kullu l-ḥiğārati tuwāfiqu li-l-ᶜamārati

Not every rock is suitable for construction

594

ليست كل سوداء فحمة ولا كل حمراء لحمة

laysat kullu sawdāᵓin faḥmatan wa-lā kullu ḥamrāᵓin laḥmatun

Not everything black is coal and not everything red is meat

All that glitters is not gold

595

ليس كل ما يعلم يقال

laysa kullu mā yuᶜlamu yuqālu

Not everything that is known should be said

596

ليس كل ما يتمنى المرء يدركه تجري الرياح بما لا
تشتهي السفن

*laysa kullu mā yatamannā l-marʾu yadrukuhu
taǧrī l-riyāhu bi-mā lā taštahī l-sufunu*

Man does not attain all his heart's desires for the winds do not blow as the vessels wish

597

ليس كل ما يلمع ذهبا

laysa kullu mā yalmaʿu ḏahaban

All is not gold that glitters

598

ليس كل مرة تسلم الجرة

laysa kullu marratin taslamu l-ǧarratu

It is not every time that the clay pot remains in a good state

A warning against pushing one's luck too far. An example is that if a person asks for a little money once a year from another, he will probably get it. If he asks too often he will not.

The pitcher goes often to the well, but is broken at last

599

ليس للحاسد إلا ما حسد

laysa li-l-ḥāsidi ʾillā mā ḥasada

The envious has nothing else than what he is envious about

600

ليس لديه وقت لحك رأسه

laysa ladayhi waqtun li-ḥakki raʾsihi

He doesn't even have time to scratch his head

Said of a very busy person.

601

ليس اليتيم الذي قد مات والده بل اليتيم يتيم العلم والأدب

laysa l-yatīmu l-laḏī qad māta wāliduhu bali l-yatīmu yatīmu l-ʿilmi wa-l-ʾadabi

He is not an orphan he whose father has died, but the orphan is the one who is an orphan of science and literature

602

الليل طويل والرب كريم

al-laylu ṭawīlun wa-l-rabbu karīmun

The night is long and God is generous

Applied to say that the matter will be solved.

حرف الميم

The letter “mīm”

603

ما محله في الإعراب؟

mā maḥalluhu fī l-ʾiʿrābi?

What is his position in syntax?

Said often with contempt about someone one finds awkward and disturbing. And who is he supposed to be?

604

ما من طائر طار وارتفع إلا كما طار وقع

mā min ṭāʾirin ṭāra wa-rtafaʿa ʾillā ka-mā ṭāra waqaʿa

No matter how high a bird flies unless as it flies it goes down

No matter how high a bird flies, it has to come down for water

605

مثل أم العروسة

miṯla ʾummi l-ʿarūsati

Like the bride's mother

Applied to a person who pretends to be very busy just to attract attention.

As busy as a hen with one chicken

606

مثل الجرس على ذنب البغل

miṯla l-ğarasi ᶜalā ḏanabi l-baġli

Like the bell on the mule's tail

Said of a very talkative person.

607

مثل الحكومة، ليس لديه صاحب

miṯla l-ḥukūmati, laysa ladayhi ṣāḥibun

Like the government, he does not have any friend

608

مثل حكاية مار بولس والعسل

miṯla ḥikāyati mār Būlus wa-l-ᶜasali

Like the story of St Paul and the honey

The proverb stems of a story that tells about a new convert who came to see St Paul to ask his advice on a legal matter. He had a jar of honey with him that he put at the feet of the saint. As St Paul has a weakness for honey, he was not able to focus on what the man was saying until he asked St Barnaby to buy the honey from the man. After that, he was able to perform his duty properly. The proverb is used when someone is trying to win a judge on his or her side.

609

مثل الحية من تحت التبن

miṯla l-ḥayyati min taḥti l-tabni

Like the snake under the hay

610

مثل خيل الدولة: اكل ومرعى وقلة صنعة

miṯla ḫayli l-dawlati: ʾaklun wa-marʿā wa-qillatu ṣanʿatin

Like the government's horse: a lot of food and recreation and doing nothing

611

مثل الزهر، يغيب سنة ويحضر شهرا

miṯla l-zahri, yaġību sanatan wa-yaḥḍaru šahran

Like the flowers, he is absent one year and present one month

Applies to a person from whom one cannot get much help.

612

مثل سفينة نوح

mit̠la safīnati Nūḥ

Like Noah's ship

Said of an ill-assorted group of people making a total mess.

613

مثل الأطرش في الزفة

mit̠la l-ʾaṭraši fī l-zaffati

Like a deaf man at a wedding procession

614

مثل غراب نوح

mit̠la ġurābi Nūḥ

Like Noah's crow

Applied to someone who is asked to fetch something and is taking a long time to come back.

615

مثل قصة إبريق الزيت

miṯla qiṣṣati ʾibrīqi l-zayti

Like the story of the oil jug

Applied to someone who is annoyed of hearing from someone else a story repeated to him with no beginning and no end. The expression originates from an anecdote that tells of someone asking someone else: “Do you want me to tell you the story of the oil jug?”. The other one answers: “Yes”. To this, the first one says: “If you said yes or if you said no, I shall tell you anyway the story of the oil jug”. So the other one says: “Like you want.” And the first one repeats the same words, saying: “Then I shall tell you the story of the oil jug. If you said yes or if you said no, I shall tell you anyway the story of the oil jug”. And the same words are repeated again and again until the other one gets irritated.

616

مثل القط بتسع ارواح

miṯla l-qitti bi-tisʿi ʾarwāhin

Like the cat that has nine lives

617

مثل الذي يوكل القط بالجبنة

mit̲la l-lad̲ī yuwakkilu l-qitta bi-l-ǧibni

Like the one who entrusts the cat with the cheese

They set the wolf to guard the sheep

618

مثل اللزقة الإنكليزية

mit̲la l-laẓqati l-ʾinklīzīyati

He is like an English plaster

Applied to someone who clings to one and whom one cannot get rid of.

619

مثل مار شليطا عينه ضيقة

mit̲la mār Šalliṭā ʿaynuhu ḍayyiqatun

Lite St Challita, his eye is narrow

Applied to someone who is stingy

620

مثل مار روكس وكلبه

mitla mār Rūks wa-kalbihi

Like St Rock and his dog

The proverb stems of a story that tells of a dog who stole bread every morning to feed St Rock in his prison. Applied to two friends who are inseparable.

621

مثل مار لورانس

mitla mār Lūrāns

Like St Lawrence

Said of someone who is angry or aggressive, like St Lawrence who was burned or "grilled" to death with the gridiron.

622

مخك في رأسك تعرف خلاصك

muḫḫuka fī raʾsika taʿrifu ḫalāṣaka

If your brain is in your head, you will know how to save yourself

623

مد رجليك على قد بساطك

midd riğlayka ʿalā qad bisāṭika

Stretch your legs according to the extent of your carpet

Cut your garment according to your cloth

<u>624</u>

مسح الأرض فيه

massaḥa l-ʾarḍa fīhi

He wiped the floor with him

Applied to a man who humiliates someone else by treating him badly.

<u>625</u>

يمسك الحبل من الطرفين

yamsiku l-ḥabla mina l-ṭarafayni

He holds the rope from both ends

Applied to someone who works for two opposite parties or who wants to be on good terms with everybody.

<u>626</u>

يمشي رويدا ويكون أولا

yamšī ruwaydan wa-yakūnu ʾawwalan

He walks slowly and arrives first

627

من أحب ولده رحم الأيتام

man ʾaḥabba waladahu raḥama l-ʾaytāma

He who loves his child is compassionate towards orphans

628

من ثمارهم سوف تعرفونهم

min ṯimārihim sawfa taʿrifūnahum

By their fruits you will know them

629

من جد وجد

man ğadda wağada

He who perseveres finds

630

من حب الخير لجاره يلقاه في داره

man ḥabba l-ḫayra li-ğārihi yalqāhu fī dārihi

He who likes that good things happen to his neighbor will find them in his own home

<u>631</u>

من حسنت سياسته دامت رئاسته

man ḥasunat siyāsatuhu dāmat riʾāsatuhu

He who governs well may govern long

<u>632</u>

من حفر حفرة لأخيه وقع فيها

man ḥafara ḥifratan li-ʾaẖīhi waqaʿa fīhā

He who digs a hole for his brother will fall in it

Hoist with his own petard i.e. blown up with his own mine

<u>633</u>

من حقر حرم

man ḥuqira ḥurima

He who was despised was deprived (of good things)

634

من خدم الرجال خدم

man ḫadama l-riǧāla ḫudima

He who serves men will be served

635

من رضي بقليله عاش

man raḍiya bi-qalīlihi ᶜāša

He who is satisfied with the little he has survives

636

من راقب الناس مات هما

man rāqaba l-nāsa māta hamman

He who watches others obsessively dies of worries

He that gazes upon the sun shall at last be blind

637

من رأى مصائب غيره هانت مصائبه

man raʾā maṣāʾiba ġayrihi hānat maṣāʾibuhu

He who sees the tragedies of others finds his own tragedies light

638

من أراد إغراق كلبه اتهمه بالجرب

man ʾarada ʾiġrāqa kalbihi ttahamahu bi-l-ǧarabi

He who wants to drown his dog says it has rabies

Give a dog a bad name and hang him

639

من زرع حصد

man zaraᶜa ḥaṣada

He who sows reaps

640

من زرع الريح حصد العاصفة

man zaraᶜa l-rīḥa ṣada l-ᶜāṣifata

He that sows the wind shall reap the whirlwind

641

من سدد ديونه نامت عيونه

man saddada duyūnahu nāmat ᶜuyūnuhu

He who has paid his debts can close his eyes to sleep

Out of debt, out of danger

642

من سنة نوح

min sanati Nūḥin

Since the year of Noah

Applied to describe something that is very old.

643

من أشترى ما لا يحتاج إليه باع ما يحتاج إليه

mani štarā mā lā yaḥtāğu ᵓilayhi bāᶜa mā yaḥtāğu ᵓilayhi

He who buys what he does not need will sell what he needs

644

من طبخ شيئا رديئا يأكل منه

man ṭabaḫa šayᵓan radīᵓan yaᵓkulu minhu

He who cooks a bad thing, eats from it

Is meant to say that the one who promotes a bad affair will suffer from it.

<u>645</u>

من طلب أخا بلا عيب بقي بلا أخ

man ṭalaba ʾaḫan bi-lā ʿaybin baqiya bi-lā ʾaḫin

He who asks for a brother without any defect remains without a brother

<u>646</u>

من طلب العلى سهر الليالي

man ṭalaba l-ʿulā sahara l-layālī

He who asks for greatness must sit up at nights

No sweet without sweat

<u>647</u>

من طلب الكثير أضاع القليل

man ṭalaba l-kaṯīra ʾaḍāʿa l-qalīla

He who asks for much loses a little

Grasp all, lose all

648

من أطاع غضبه ضيع أدبه

man ʾaṭāʿa ġaḍabahu ḍayyaʿa ʾadabahu

He who obeys his anger loses his manners

649

من ظلم ظلم

man ẓalama ẓulima

He who treats others unfairly will be treated unfairly

650

من عاشر الفحام وسخ ثيابه

man ʿāšara l-faḥḥāma wassaḫa ṯiyābahu

He who frequents the stoker dirties his clothes

651

من عمل دائما أكل نائما

man ʿamala dāʾiman ʾakala nāʾiman

He who works all day eats while sleeping

Applied to express the utility of working.

652

من أعانك على الشر ظلمك

man ʾaʿānaka ʿalā l-šarri ẓalamaka

The one who helped you in doing evil has treated you unjustly

653

من كثر إحسانه كثر إخوانه

man kaṯura ʾiḥsānuhu kaṯura ʾiḫwānuhu

He whose good deeds are many has many brothers

654

من كثر ضحكه قلت هيبته

man kaṯura ḍiḥkuhu qallat haybatuhu

As laughter increases, respect decreases

The loud laugh bespeaks the vacant mind

655

من كذب مرة كذب كل مرة

man kaḏḏaba marratan kaḏḏaba kulla marratin

He who lies once lies every time

656

من تكلم بما لا يعنيه سمع ما لا يرضيه

man takallama bi-mā lā yaᶜnīhi samiᶜa mā lā yarḍīhi

He who talks about what does not concern him will hear what does not please him

657

من لا يصلحه الخير لا يصلحه الشر

man lā yuṣalliḥuhu l-ḫayru lā yuṣalliḥuhu l-šarru

He whom goodness cannot correct, evil cannot correct either

Said of an incorrigible person.

658

من لم يحسن إلى نفسه لم يحسن إلى غيره

man lam yuḥsin ᵓilā nafsihi lam yuḥsin ᵓilā ġayrihi

He who does not do well to himself will not do well to others

659

من لم يرض بحكم موسى يرضي بحكم فرعون

*man lam yarḍa bi-ḥikmi Mūsā yarḍī bi-ḥikmi
Farᶜūna*

*He who is not satisfied with Moses' government
will be satisfied with Pharaoh's government*

Is meant to say that the one who does not accept a
mild government will have to accept a tyrannical one.

660

من وعظ أخاه سرا فقد نصحه ومن وعظه علانية فقد
فضحه

*man waᶜaẓa ʾaḫāhu sirran fa-qad naṣaḥahu, wa-
man waᶜaẓahu ᶜalānīyatan fa-qad faḍaḥahu*

*He who preaches to his brother in private
advises him, he who preaches to him publicly
exposes him*

661

مات كلب الأمير، كل الناس عزت فيه

مات الأمير لم يهتم أحد فيه

māta kalbu l-ʾamīri, kullu l-nāsi ᶜazzat fīhi

māta l-ʾamīru lam yahtam ʾaḥadun fīhi

When the Emir's dog died, everyone sent their condolences; when the Emir himself died, no one paid any attention to him

662

الموت ولا المذلة

al-mawtu wa-lā l-maḏallatu

Better to die than to suffer of shame

663

ماله مصون وعرضه مبتذل

māluhu maṣūnun wa-ʿirḍuhu mubtaḏalun

His wealth is preserved and his honor is held in mean estimation

حرف النون

The letter "nūn"

664

النجوم في السماء أقرب إليك

al-nuğūmu fī l-samāʾi ʾaqrabu ʾilayka

The stars in the sky are closer to you

Said to someone whose aim in a mission is impossible to achieve.

665

نحن في التفكير والله في التدبير

naḥnu fī l-tafkīri wa-l-lāhu fī l-tadbīri

Man proposes and God disposes

666

نحن في وادي وأنتم في وادي

naḥnu fī wādī wa-ʾantum fī wādī

We are in a valley and you are in a valley

Is meant to say that we are separated geographically or by different life styles or wavelengths.

667

نحن في دمشق وأنتم في عمان

naḥnu fī Dimašq wa-ᵓantum fī ᶜAmmān

We are in Damascus and you are in Amman

This is a variant of the proverb above (661).

668

نحن مثل الأعصار نبدأ بحماس ونخلص بكارثة

naḥnu miṯla l-ᵓaᶜṣāri nabdaᵓu bi-ḥamāsin wa-naḫlaṣu bi-kāriṯatin

We are like the hurricanes, we start with enthusiasm and end up in a disaster

669

تنسى خالقها ولا تنسى مطلقها

tansā ḫāliqahā wa-lā tansā muṭalliqahā

She forgets her Creator but she does not forget the one who divorced her

670

نصف العلم أخطر من الجهل

niṣfu l-ᶜilmi ᵓaḫṭaru mina l-ǧahli

Half a learning is more dangerous than ignorance

A little learning is a dangerous thing

<u>671</u>

منتظر الفرج

muntaẓiru l-faraği

He is waiting for freedom from grief

<u>672</u>

أنظف من الصحن الصيني

ᵓanẓafu mina l-ṣaḥni l-Ṣīnī

Cleaner than the Chinese plate

<u>673</u>

النعجة الجرباء تعدي كل القطيع

al-naᶜğatu l-ğarbāᵓu taᶜdī kulla l-qaṭīᶜi

The scabby sheep contaminates the whole flock

<u>674</u>

الناس أتباع من غلب

al-nāsu ʾatbāʿu man ġalaba

People are the followers of he who wins

Like master, like man

675

الناس على دين ملوكهم

al-nāsu ʿalā dīni mulūkihim

People follow their kings' religion

Like master, like man

676

ينام مع الدجاج

yanāmu maʿa l-dağāği

He sleeps when the chickens go to sleep

Applied to someone who sleeps very early.

677

النوم سلطان

al-nawmu sulṭānun

Sleep is a sultan

Applied to express the benefit of sleep.

678

النوم في كدر ولا رقود تحت الحجر

al-nawmu fī kadarin wa-lā ruqūdun taḥta l-ḥağari

It is better to sleep in the mud than to sleep under the stone

حرف الهاء

The letter "hāʾ"

679

هم يبكي وهم يضحك

hammun yubakkī wa-hammun yuḍaḥḥiku

One woe makes one cry and one woe makes one laugh

680

هو بهذا عالم بيطار

huwa bi-hāḏā ʿālimun bayṭār

He is knowing and skillful in this matter

681

هو كالكمأة لا أصل ثابت ولا فرع نابت

huwa ka-l-kamʾati lā āṣlun ṯābitun wa-lā firʿun nābitun

He's like a potatoes plant; no steady roots and no branches growing

حرف الواو

The letter “wāw”

682

وبعض القول يذهب في الرياح

And some words go with the winds

683

وما اللذة إلا بعد التعب

wa-mā l-liddatu ʾillā baʿda l-taʿabi

Pleasure is not reached unless after endeavor

684

وجهه يقطع الرزق

wağhuhu yaqṭaʿu l-rizqa

His face cuts off all gains

685

وجهه مثل ورقة النعوة

wağhuhu mitla waraqati l-naʿwati

His face is like a death notice

<u>686</u>

الوحدة خير من جليس السوء

al-waḥdatu ḫayrun min ǧalīsi l-sūʾi

Better be alone than in bad company

<u>687</u>

واحد حامل ذقنه والثاني تعبان فيها

wāḥidun ḥāmilun ḏaqnahu wa-l-ṯānī taʿbānun fīhā

One is carrying his chin (beard) and the second one is tired with it

Applies to a person who carries others' worries without gaining anything.

<u>688</u>

الاتحاد أساس النجاح

al-ʾittiḥādu ʾasāsu l-naǧāḥi

Union is the foundation of success

<u>689</u>

الإتحاد قوة

al-ʾittiḥādu quwwatun

Union is strength

United we stand, divided we fall

690

وراء كل رجل عظيم إمرأة

warāʾa kulli rağulin ʿaẓīmin ʾimratun

Behind every great man there is a woman

691

يضع سره في أضعف خلقه

yaḍaʿu sirrahu fī ʾaḍʿafi ḫilqihi

He (God) puts His secrets in the weakest of His creation

692

ضع يدك في وكر الدبابير وقل هذا من التقادير

ḍaʿ yadaka fī wakri l-dabābīri wa-qul hāḏā mina l-taqādīri

Put your hand in a hornet's nest and say this is my fate

Applied to someone who does stupid things and blames his faith for the consequences.

693

وعد الحر دين عليه

waʿdu l-ḥurri dīnun ʿalayhi

The free man's promise is a debt to him

*A promise is a debt that we must not
forget*

694

إتفق القط والفأر على خرب الدار

ʾittafaqa l-qiṭṭu wa-l-faʾru ʿalā ḫarbi l-dāri

*The cat and the mouse agreed to destroy the
house*

Applied to describe a situation in which enemies
have allied themselves against a third party.

695

الوقت أثمن من الذهب

al-waqtu ʾaṯmanu mina l-ḏahabi

Time is more precious than gold

696

الوقت كالسيف إن لم تقطعه قطعك

al-waqtu ka-l-sayfi ʾin lam taqṭaʿhu qaṭaʿaka

Time is like a sword. If you do not cut it, it will cut you

<u>697</u>

الوقت من الذهب

al-waqtu mina l-ḏahabi

Time is gold

Time is money

<u>698</u>

واقع بين نارين

wāqiʿun bayna nārayni

Fallen between two fires

<u>699</u>

الولد ولد ولو حكم بلدا

al-waladu waladun wa-law ḥakama baladan

The child is a child even if he governs a country

700

ولدك ولدك ليوم زواجه وبنتك بنتك طول حياتها

waladuki waladuki li-yawmi zawāğihi wa-bintuki bintuki ṭūla ḥayātihā

Your son is your son until his wedding day, your daughter is your daughter all her life

A son is a son till he takes him a wife, a daughter is a daughter all her life

حرف الياء

The letter "yāᵓ"

701

يا أيها الجبل العالي لا يهزك ريح

yā ᵓayyuhā l-ğabalu l-ᶜāliyu lā yahizzuka rīhun

O you high mountain, no wind moves you!

Said of someone who always remains calm and stoic in the face of hardships.

702

يا رب لا تجعلني عبرة لغيري

yā rabbu la tağᶜalnī ᶜibratan li-ġayrī

O God, do not make me an example to others

703

يا صبر أيوب

yā ṣabra ᵓayyūba

O Job's patience!

Said of someone who has many trials like Job did.

704

يا طالب الدبس من النمس

yā ṭāliba l-dibsi mina l-nimsi

O you who ask for molasses from a weasel

Said of someone who expects good things from a bad person.

705

يا ليت الشباب يعود يوما فأخبره بما فعل المشيب

yā layta l-šabāba
yaᶜūdu yawman fa-ʾuḫbiruhu bi-mā faᶜala l-mušību

O I wish that youth returned so that I will tell to it what the aging man has done

706

يد واحدة لا تصفق

yadun wāḥidatun lā tuṣaffiqu

One hand alone cannot clap

Applied to say that people should cooperate to get things done.

There is no "I" in team

707

يده بركة

yaduhu barakatun

His hand is a blessing

Is said of a kind and generous person.

708

يده خفيفة

yaduhu ḫafīfatun

His hand is light

Is said for instance of a nurse who is clever in giving an injection or of a thief who is clever at stealing.

709

يده طويلة

yaduhu ṭawīlatun

His hand is long

Is said of a thief.

710

الإيمان يزحزح الجبال

al-ʾimānu yuzaḥziḥu l-ǧibāla

Faith moves mountains

711

يوم السرور قصير

yawmu l-surūri qaṣīrun

The day of happiness is short

712

يوم عسل ويوم بصل

yawmu ʿasalin wa-yawmu baṣalin

A day of honey and a day of onion

Some days are diamonds, some are stones

CPSIA information can be obtained at www.ICGtesting.com
Printed in the USA
BVOW03s1443020816

457528BV00001BA/21/P

9 789197 895453